CORPORATE INTERIORS

CORPORATE INTERIORS

Corporate Interiors Design Book Series No. 1

McGraw-Hill, Inc.

New York   San Francisco   Washington, D.C.   Auckland   Bogotá   Caracas   Lisbon
London   Madrid   Mexico City   Milan   Montreal   New Delhi   San Juan
Singapore   Sydney   Tokyo   Toronto

Retail Reporting Corporation
302 Fifth Avenue
New York, NY 10001

Distributors to the trade in the United States and Canada
McGraw-Hill, Inc.
1221 Avenue of the Americas
New York, NY 10020

Distributors outside the United States and Canada
Hearst Books International
1350 Avenue of the Americas
New York, NY 10019

Library of Congress Cataloging in Publication Data:
Corporate Interiors

Printed in Hong Kong
IISBN 0-07-018243-4

Book Design: Harish Patel Design Associates

CONTENTS

Introduction

This is a rare book. What Lester Dundes, my old friend and Interior Design magazine's longtime publisher, has put together is something the design field — and those interested in it — have long needed. While the newsstands, the newspapers, and the bookshops sag under the weight of books and articles about residential interior design, coverage of the corporate (or "commercial," or — to use a slightly broader term — "contract") interior design field is almost entirely limited to professional magazines.

It's strange that this should be so, for, although the importance of residential design to our personal comfort, security, and happiness can hardly be overrated, the importance of contract design is at least as important. Most of us probably spend more of our waking hours in contract environments than in residential ones. We work in contract spaces, and because "the office" is the most familiar category, this book gives it a primary focus, but offices are just the tip of the iceberg. We eat in restaurants and cafés, then work off the results in salons and gyms; we spend our money in shops and stores, then try to forget our bills in theaters and movie houses, while trying to avoid institutions such as hospitals and jails; we travel from airports and terminals via planes and trains to inns and hotels, so we can visit galleries and museums (and more restaurants and cafés). All these facilities and more have interiors that are the work of contract designers.

An odd term, contract design, but it's one that has stuck. In the older, simpler days of fifty years ago or so, all one needed to do in order to become a residential designer was to have some cards printed up, assume an appropriate attitude, and (if female) secure an excellent hat. The furnishings and fabrics that went into the residential jobs were then selected and (usually) purchased by the designer, piece by fabulous piece. No contract. When it became widely apparent that office, commercial, and institutional interiors also needed design attention, a different basis of working developed, in which large numbers of desks or chairs or large amounts of fabric or carpeting were contracted for and bought en masse.

One implication of contract design is the method in which payment is made. In the old days (and, to some extent, even today) residential designers were paid for the merchandise they provided, their profits coming from markups on that merchandise. That is virtually never the case for contract designers, who are paid on the basis of their time, or of the scope and difficulty of the job, or of some prearranged fee.

There are other differences. All interior design these days is conducted on a more professional level than in the past, but contract design is necessarily even more professional than residential. The interior of a house or apartment is used by its occupant, family and invited friends, but the interior of an office, theater, airport, or shopping center is used not only by those who work there but also by many who were not necessarily either invited or friends. Obviously, our government feels it must protect our citizens in such environments, and a complex tangle of rules for safety, security, and accessibility must apply. It is one of the contract designer's chief tasks to untangle and properly apply those rules.

Another task is to understand and properly employ a whole cornucopia of new materials and techniques, a cornucopia that never stops flowing. To take the selection of carpet as one of many possible examples, the choice is no longer just wool, synthetic, or a blend of both. There are decisions to be made about dyeing, printing, weaving, tufting, knitting, or carving the carpet. There is a choice of broadloom or carpet tile. There are the questions of padding, underlays, and installation. There are considerations of fire resistance, abrasion resistance, and ease of maintenance. The cost must be appropriate, and delivery must be properly timed. And — oh, yes - what it looks like must also be considered.

And that growing professionalism we alluded to? Increasingly, design education is being strictly monitored, with four-year degree-granting institutions now the norm, their curricula accredited by the Foundation for Interior Design Education Research, and with some schools offering further study and a master's degree. Increasingly, state legislatures, realizing a design's impact on the health, safety, and welfare of its users, are requiring education, experience, and the passage of a really tough examination, administered by the National Council for Interior Design Qualification, in order for the title Interior Designer to be used. And increasingly, interior design professional organizations are unifying to create fewer, stronger groups and demanding higher qualifications for membership. That excellent hat no longer does the trick.

Such heightened professionalism is made manifest in work such as the examples shown in this book. Without such professionalism, the interiors illustrated could not have succeeded at solving the problems they faced, including problems of space utilization, efficiency, communication, and productivity. With or without the hat, today's contract interior design is immeasurably more than just a pretty face. But even more remarkable is the fact that, while solving those serious and quite concrete problems, the design firms that participated in this book have also addressed the equally serious but less tangible problems of creating interiors that are visually appropriate, agreeable, uplifting, and even beautiful. This is not only a rare type of book; it's a book packed with rare talent.

Stanley Abercrombie, FAIA, Hon. FASID, Hon. IIDA

Preface

This book is a sampler of some of the best work currently being generated in the field of corporate design. The 33 design firms invited to participate were chosen from the most important and respected practitioners in the field. Each of them chose two, three, or even four of their recent commissions that they considered representative of their best efforts. In all, over a hundred projects are shown, most of them in the United States, a few abroad. The resultant collection, arranged alphabetically by firm name, gives, an overview of what is happening today in corporate design and in related types of commercial and institutional design. But the collection does not — cannot — show the whole picture, not even for the 33 firms represented, for every good design firm has a variety of skills and is capable of working in a variety of styles and solving a variety of problems. It would take a long shelf of 33 hefty volumes to show everything these designers are able to do.

Two essays complete our book. The first, by Stanley Abercrombie, longtime editor-inchief of *Interior Design* magazine, explains what corporate designers do and how their work differs from that of residential designers. The second, by designer and educator Mike Tatum, gives practical advice about how to select and hire a design firm. Finally, taking a tip from the design magazines, where ad pages receive as much interested readership as editorial pages, we have allowed a few manufacturers (for a price) to display some of the products that are now being made for use in corporate interiors.

Together, we hope these elements combine to shed a clarifying light on the character, accomplishment, and range of the corporate interior today.

LESTER DUNDES

8

Architectural Resources Cambridge, Inc. (ARC)

140 Mount Auburn Street
Cambridge
MA 02138
617.547.2200
617.547.7222 (Fax)

Architectural Resources Cambridge, Inc. (ARC)

Lotus Development Corporation Headquarters Cambridge, Massachusetts

Growth and change were both expected when Lotus asked ARC to design its new 250,000-square-foot corporate headquarters and sales offices in Cambridge. Heavy electronics use and consequently heavy power and air conditioning needs were also factors to be accommodated, with a work environment averaging more than one personal computer per employee and relying on data links and sophisticated telephone capabilities. Yet a sense of stability and permanence was also provided by means of accumulated details such as mahogany-framed glass office fronts, a coffered ceiling and large mahogany desk in the reception area, mahogany column trim, indirect cove lighting, and colonnaded corridors. Sales training and conference rooms have been given direct access from the reception area, but an offset corridor and a lighted niche signal the end of the public space and provide privacy to the office functions beyond.

Below: Reception and guest waiting area.
Opposite, above: Conference room, with view to waiting area.
Opposite, right, center: Corner office and meeting room.
Opposite, left, below: Executive office.
Photography: Nick Wheeler

Architectural Resources Cambridge, Inc. (ARC)

University of Iowa
John Pappajohn Business Administration Building
Iowa City, Iowa

Designed to consolidate the Business College facilities previously scattered throughout the University of Iowa campus, this 187,000-square-foot, four-floor building provides classrooms, conference rooms, computer rooms, offices, a behavioral laboratory, a library, and a 450-seat auditorium. Accommodated here are 1,300 BA candidates, 650 MBA candidates, and 150 PhD candidates, as well as the faculty, with undergraduates in one wing, graduates in another, and library, computer center, and administration where the wings meet. A below-grade garage provides parking for 126 cars. The scale and character of the building are sympathetic to its context, which includes Iowa's original state capitol, a limestone structure built in 1849, and the copper-clad towers of Gilmore Hall, another landmark.

Above: *Entrance gate and portico.*
Right: *High-ceilinged meeting room in the fourth floor penthouse.*
Below: *Classroom with stepped tiers of seating.*
Photography: *Nick Wheeler*

Above: *A dramatic composition of stairs.*
Right: *The sun-filled central atrium.*

Architectural Resources Cambridge, Inc. (ARC)

Ciba Corning Diagnostics
East Walpole, Massachusetts

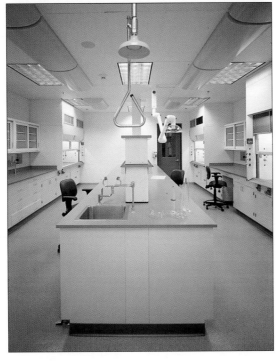

Opposite, above:
Exterior view.
Opposite, below:
Reception lobby walls
have wood battens that
recall the joints in the
building's metal-paneled
facade; flooring is ter-
razzo.

Left, above: View into
atrium.
Above: Skylit circulation
spine.
Left: Laboratory area.
Photography:
Exterior: Nick Wheeler.
Interiors: John Horner.

Ciba Corning manufac-
tures a broad range of
diagnostic reagents and
clinical instruments. ARC
was hired in 1991 to
develop a master plan
for the company and to
design a research, devel-
opment, and production
facility. Recently the firm
was called back to
expand the facility with
an 89,000-square-foot
addition for research and
a 190,000-square-foot
addition for production.

Within the research addi-
tion, laboratories are
consolidated in the cen-
ter of the building, giv-
ing these specialized
environments the strin-
gent controls they
require -- separate air
systems and filters, pres-
sure differentials, air
locks, ducted fume
hoods, clean rooms, lim-
ited access corridors, and
a variety of water supply
and waste piping sys-
tems. Surrounding the

laboratories, perimeter
offices enjoy natural
light, and light also pen-
etrates the laboratory
core through skylights
and glazed atria. The
modularity of the lab
design will facilitate
future changes in use,
and a full basement
affords easy access for
maintenance and build-
ing system upgrades.

Architectural Resources Cambridge, Inc. (ARC)

Case Western Reserve University
Dively Executive Education Center
Cleveland, Ohio

The executive education programs of the Weatherhead School of Management have recently been consolidated in the Dively Center. The 38,000-square-foot structure, designed by ARC, includes 50-person and 100-person lecture rooms, a 50-person electronic learning classroom, a 200-seat dining room, a library and reading room, lounges, and administrative offices. The heart of the Dively Center, however, is the Pavilion, a double-height space with high arched windows and a grand staircase; it can accommodate more than 200 people for lectures, banquets, or receptions, and it also offers seating and study alcoves and break-out areas for the adjoining meeting rooms and classrooms; its doors open to a ter-race for outdoor receptions. Fiber optic and data hook-ups are located throughout the space. In addition, the Hanson Board Room offers a modular conference table, intimate seating alcoves, a classically detailed fireplace, and audio/visual capabilities. In all, ARC's Dively Center combines the welcoming atmosphere of a large house with state-of-the-art learning and teaching technology.

Above:
Building exterior.
Right: *The Pavilion's grand stair.*
Below: *The Hanson Board Room.*
Photography: *Eric Hanson*

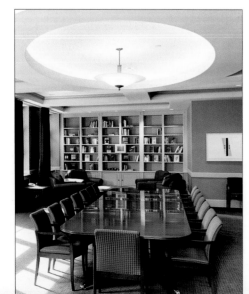

Berger Rait Design Associates, Inc.

20 Exchange Place
28th Floor
New York
NY 10005
212.742.7000
212.742.7001 (Fax)

Berger Rait Design Associates, Inc.

Below: Sliding doors at left can enclose conference room.

Berger Rait Offices
New York, New York

A design firm's design for its own quarters reveals a great deal about the firm's priorities and ideals as well as about its talents. Berger Rait's own offices occupy 5,000 square feet of the 28th floor of a Lower Manhattan tower. What the firm accomplished (at the enviably small cost of $30 a square foot) is a paradigm of open planning and consequently easy communication. Only the conference room is an enclosed, private space, while all staff members, including the firm's principals, share open quarters. The result, reportedly, is that if a change occurs in a particular design scheme, "all the team members are immediately aware of that change." In the main drafting area, a central island holds plan files and lateral files, its top surface in constant use for design presentations and reviews. Wrapping around the island is the firm's extensive resource library. South-facing windows enjoy a river view, and French doors lead to a small balcony.

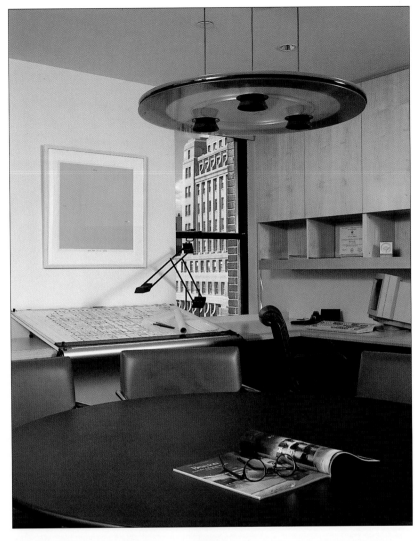

Right: A partner's work station.
Below, right: Drafting room with resource library at left.
Below, left: Conference room.
Photography: Elliot Fine

Berger Rait Design Associates, Inc.

Below: *Reception and waiting area.*
Bottom of page: *Corner executive office.*
Photography: *Paul Warchol*

Executive Offices
New York, New York

This suite of offices is in a privileged location: the 33rd floor of a tower at Madison Avenue and 57th Street in Manhattan, with Central Park views from the corner windows. Requirements were offices for an executive and his staff, including support areas, conference rooms, and an executive bath. The executive's office was given the prime corner location, with other offices along the perimeter walls, but with glass fronts to allow light penetration to interior work areas. A special request for extra ceiling height was accommodated by re-routing overhead mechanical systems. To focus attention on the executive's collection of art and artifacts, finishes were kept light and neutral. Cost for the 5,000 square feet was $500,000.

Above: Conference room.
Right: Another view of reception area.

Berger Rait Design Associates, Inc.

Sullivan & Liapakis, P.C.
New York, New York

The 60-year-old New York law firm of Sullivan & Liapakis is the largest plaintiffs personal injury litigation firm in the country. In 1995 it celebrated two milestone events: partner Pamela Liapakis became president of the Association of Trial Lawyers of America, and the firm moved into 45,000 square feet of Manhattan's historic 1912 Equitable Life Building, more than doubling its previous space. The traditional image devised by Berger Rait is appropriate for both the firm and the building. Housed here are the firm's 16 partners and 24 associates, grouped in nine legal specialties and with an unusually large need for conference rooms. There are five such rooms, all different in size, shape, and table configuration, and all linked by French doors of cherry and glass, so that, conjoined, they can double as space for entertaining. Equally impressive is the 1,000-square-foot reception area, welcoming visitors with Oriental carpets and cutom millwork. A gym is also on the premises, and all work stations are wired for PCs and networked.

Above: *Entrance with identifying graphics.*
Below: *French doors link two conference rooms.*
Opposite: *The large wood-paneled reception area.*
Photography: *Elliot Fine*

Left: A rectangular conference room

Below, left: An oval conference room.

Below, right: View into a partner,s office.

Brennan Beer Gorman Monk / Interiors

515 Madison Avenue
New York
NY 10022
212.888.7667
212.935.3868 (Fax)

1250 24 Street, Suite 250
Washington, DC
20037
202.452.1644
202.452.1647 (Fax)

13/F Lyndhurst Tower
1 Lyndhurst Terrace
Central, Hong Kong
852.2525.9766
852.2525.9850 (Fax)

Brennan Beer Gorman Monk / Interiors

IAM National Pension Fund
Washington, DC

The International Association of Machinists' National Pension Fund has relocated to 34,000 square feet on three contiguous floors of a 12-floor Washington office building. On one of the avenues cutting diagonally through the city's street grid, the building was oddly shaped, with irregularly spaced columns and asymmetrical core elements. The design solution has capitalized on these conditions, using them to create niches for art work and small "jewel box" conference rooms. The building's mechanical system was upgraded to meet the demands of new technology, and, because operations here are paper-intensive and a concentrated storage area was needed, structural reinforcement was added as well.

Reception and executive areas are located on the building's third floor, with most of the IAM's 12 departments on floors above and below. The executive area, also on the third floor, focuses on a 30-by-40-foot conference room designed for 40-person Board of Trustee meetings. Materials here include stone flooring inset with carpet, and elements of brushed and polished steel serve as references to the work of machinists.

Above: Entrance and reception area.
Right: Corridor with glass-walled office.
Opposite, above: An executive office.
Opposite, below: The IAM boardroom.
Photography: Dan Cunningham

Right:
The IAM boardroom.

Brennan Beer Gorman Monk / Interiors

Parsons Brinckerhoff
Corporate Headquarters
New York, New York

Above: *Elevator lobby, with view to reception area.*
Below: *Boardroom.*

Right: *Stair and bas-relief mural.*
Photography: *Peter Paige*

The interior design of Parsons Brinckerhoff's new world headquarters is a celebration of the engineering firm's hundred-year history and is meant to position the firm for its next hundred. It occupies 125,000 square feet on two floors. The client's corporate identity is first established in the elevator lobby, where a canted wall faced with eucalyptus veneer is topped by a vault of machine-brushed sheet metal. Beyond electronically monitored glass doors, the reception area is visible. This two-story space is dominated by a curved 20-by-35-foot mural composed of 11 plaster bas-relief panels depicting the firm's interna-

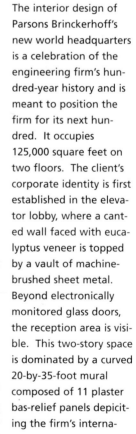

tional achievements with bridges, tunnels, and highways. The adjacent stair has an open railing of hand-brushed bronze. The installation also includes a boardroom with state-of-the-art electronics, 11 other conference and training rooms, 450 work stations, an employee food service area, and, next to it, an open lounge for informal meetings.

Above: Reliefs illustrate engineering feats in Parsons Brinckerhoff's history. In this one, William Barclay Parsons surveys the first railroad route between Hankow and Canton.
Right: Corridor with canted photo grids and bronze ceiling canopies.

Design Collective Incorporated

130 East Chestnut Street
Columbus
OH 43215
614.464.2880
614.464.1180 (Fax)

1701 East 12th Street
Cleveland
OH 44114
216.771.2880
216.771.1058 (Fax)

222 Second Avenue North
Suite 100
Nashville
TN 37201
615.242.7382
615.254.4613 (Fax)

Design Collective Incorporated

Sterling Commerce is a computer software and information exchange company with offices throughout the United States. The campus for its administrative offices, in Dublin, Ohio, has three buildings totaling 250,000 square feet. The one shown here connects to all the company facilities through video conferencing rooms, and its board room also has extensive high-tech capabilities for connection to other Sterling locations. The building's lobby is an interactive space where visitors, customers, and trainees view monitors, integrated with the interior design, that show computer-generated images and data about Sterling's products as well as endorsements from clients. From the lobby, there is access to an expansive meeting room used daily for training on software and interactive systems. Also nearby is a full-service kitchen serving lunches and break beverages; it connects via dumbwaiter to the third floor's executive board room and dining room. Adding a final note of enlightenment, each of Sterling's three buildings has been given its own distinctive art program.

Right: In the lobby, visitors are greeted by monitors imbedded in a curved wall.
Photography: *StudiOhio*

Design Collective Incorporated

Pizzuti Inc.
Columbus, Ohio

Pizzuti Inc., a major developer and real estate entrepreneur in the Columbus area, was a satisfied client of Design Collective Incorporated a decade ago. Recently Pizzuti returned, asking the same firm to redesign the space "but even better." An additional area for the accounting and real estate departments was connected with an internal stair, bringing the total area to 23,500 square feet, and Ron Pizzuti's own office was enlarged and rearranged, but the major work was to inject a new design experience. The space was recarpeted and recolored to reflect the lighter, clearer color palette of the 1990s. In the reception area, a rather monumental, monolithic desk was replaced by a more lightly scaled stainless steel structure faced with hand-patinated copper sleeves supporting a sheet of sand-etched glass, and the space was also given new furniture, flower pedestals and artwork. Perhaps the next decade will bring further changes by DCI that will again be "even better."

Left: Custom reception desk is fronted by a structure of glass and copper. Special uplighting, recessed in the floor, adds further drama.
Below: The private office of Ron Pizzuti.
Photography: StudiOhio

Design Collective Incorporated

Chordant is the product distribution division of a large music company, EMI Christian Music Group, whose diverse product ranges from classic gospel to heavy-metal praise music. Its 3,000-square-foot quarters in Nashville have been designed by Design Collective Incorporated for only $35. per square foot. They include a reception area, eight offices with support space, and a multi-media product presentation room. This last room's custom board table has power connections to large-screen audio/visual sophisticated equipment behind maple pocket doors. A large sliding door of aluminum and maple introduces a touch of warehouse imagery, but the company's logo of concentric rings, interpreted in custom carpeting, adds a softer, more playful effect.

Right: The company's upscale product presentation room is designed to appeal to a younger listening audience.
Photography:
Robert Ames Cook

38

Design Collective Incorporated

The challenge here, in offices for a law firm with an expanding labor relations practice, was to create an environment respecting the traditional image of an attorney's office, but to also reflect the fresher, brighter quality of today's best work environments. The client's collection of antique furniture had to be accommodated, and new furniture and fabrics were chosen to complement it, but the designers also chose a palette of light, neutral colors that gives a visual lift to the traditional elements. Two particular focal points of the 8,000-square-foot space were the reception area and the entrance to the law library, and both areas have been given porticos beneath pyramidal coves, with both the coves and the columns given dramatic custom lighting effects; there are also central pendant lighting fixtures and marble floors. Despite such touches of traditional elegance, the cost was held to $38. per square foot.

Right: Columned entrance to the law firm's reception area.
Photography: Robert Ames Cook

Design Collective Incorporated

Design Collective Incorporated's own offices
Columbus, Cleveland, and Nashville

Design Collective Incorporated has a total staff of approximately thirty distributed in offices in Columbus, Cleveland, and Nashville. The 2,000-square-foot Cleveland office, seen at right, is on the ground floor of a 22-story mixed-use downtown building, a highly visible location, and the design goal was to make a space attractive enough to work as a marketing tool, but on a budget limited to the tenant finish allowance of $80,000. The 4,000-square-foot Nashville office, below left, is a spiritedly contemporary design within a highly traditional Historic Register building. Another prominent location; its central entrance leads directly to the chief conference room beyond pivoting glass doors; and its bud-

get was $35. a square foot. The 5,000-square-foot Columbus, Ohio, office (below, right) is the largest and oldest of the three branches and was built for the similarly modest sum of $157,000, including all services. Because the DCI firm offers graphic design as well as interior design services, and because the firm strongly believes that humor is a desirable element to add to any work environment, playful graphic solutions have been devised, including bold primary colors and an imaginative use of curved forms. The result in each of the three cities is economical and energetic and has reportedly attracted a number of new clients for Design Collective Incorporated.

Harley Ellington Design

26913 Northwestern
Highway, Suite 200
Southfield
MI 48034
810.262.1500
810.262.1515 (Fax)
http://www.hedesign.com

Harley Ellington Design

Comerica Incorporated
Operations Center Renovation
Auburn Hills, Michigan

Above: General work area.
Right: Path in carpet leads from public area to work area.
Opposite: Window openings of various size betwen corridor and work area.
Photography: Gary Quesada, Korab Hedrich Blessing

Following the recent merger of two Detroit-area banks, Comerica, Inc., and Manufacturer's Bank, this former check processing facility needed to be thoroughly overhauled and transformed into a service center. Paper handling chores were to be replaced by problem solving tasks, the "office factory" image by a more professional one. Harley Ellington Design, having planned the earlier facility in 1994, was invited back to mastermind the conversion. The result is 405,000 gross square feet of highly ordered and efficient space, brightened and made comprehensible by color codings and carpet patterns that double as pathfinding aids. The lighting design, selected with the clients and their construction managers on the basis of a number of alternative mock-ups, is a carefully considered blend of natural and artificial, the latter reflected from nine-foot-high ceilings.

Left: Conference room with glass wall.
Below: Two views of corridors ringing the four-story atrium.
Opposite: Lounge area centered in the atrium.

Harley Ellington Design

Below: *Conference room with a view.*
Bottom of page: *Entrance to the facility.*
Photography: *Gary Quesada, Korab Hedrich Blessing*

Renaissance Conference Center
Renaissance Center
Detroit, Michigan

Serving not only the tenants of Detroit's Renaissance Center complex, but also other downtown businesses, this is a flexibility-foremost facility providing meeting space for up to 280 visitors. Its main area is divisible into three smaller areas and is supplemented by two additional rooms seating from 12 to 24. All meeting spaces are served by computerized lighting controls, multiple camera locations for videoconferencing, a voice lift system for audience participation, and a super-quiet mechanical system to preserve acoustic clarity. Supporting areas include the reception/lobby area, break-out areas, a management office, and a full-service kitchen, bringing the total area to almost 11,000 square feet. Furniture with cherry veneers and fabrics in deep, rich colors were chosen to avoid an institutional look.

46

Right: Room with desks and video monitors.
Below: Another area with movable seating.

Harley Ellington Design

Below, left: *The 1,000-seat dining facility.*
Below, right: *View into a conference room.*
Bottom of page: *Serving area for the dining facility.*
Photography: *Gary Quesada, Korab Hedrich Blessing*

General Motors Corporation Truck Product Center Pontiac, Michigan

With a building footprint equal to 16 football fields, this Harley Ellington Design solution provides offices and research/development space for 4,200 GM engineers and support personnel, consolidated here after previously being scattered in 11 other locations. But the initial manufacturing complex on the site, built in the 1930s and now obsolete, was even larger. Harley Ellington Design's assignment included master planning of the surrounding 270-acre business campus, and their studies mandated demolition of much of the earlier construction. The building shown here was retained but totally transformed with new metal and glass exterior sheathing, new security systems, 2,000 miles of new electrical and communications cabling, five linear miles of light fixtures, a reworked mechanical system, and 14 miles of Herman Miller workstation partitions.

Environetics Group

215 Park Avenue South
New York
NY 10003
212.260.9060
212.260.1505 (Fax)

Environetics Group

The Durst Organization
New York, New York

The Durst Organization, a third-generation family business, is one of New York's major real estate owners and developers. Recent work by Environetics Group relocated the company from a space it had occupied for twenty years into new 20,000-square-foot quarters on a single floor of a company-owned building, 1155 Avenue of the Americas. The character wanted by Durst was not necessarily traditional, but was still corporate and substantial. Contemporary details were therefore employed, but in solid natural materials such as stone and wood. A lively and communicative touch, seen in the reception area, conference areas, and other public spaces, is a series of three-dimensional displays incorporating photographic images of Durst properties. For these displays and throughout the installation, lighting systems using both fluorescent and halogen fixtures create carefully calculated effects. Four conference areas, in varying sizes, were created, with a serving kitchen located nearby.

Opposite: Custom work
stations for the secretarial staff face doors to private offices.
Above: Board room.
Service alcove at left
provides direct access
from kitchen area.
Left: Adjacent to the
board room, a small cau-
cus area that can be
closed off with motor-
ized recessed sliding
panels.

Environetics Group

Rubin, Baum, Levin, Constant & Friedman
New York, New York

For a medium-sized law firm with a number of senior partners, this location on one and a half floors in the premiere building of New York's Rockefeller Center was, in some ways, ideal: a prestigious location and a floor plan offering opportunities for eight corner offices per floor. But the 1930s construction predated modern requirements for computer cabling and electrical and mechanical equipment. Equipping the 40,000 square feet with the latest technology therefore needed considerable attention to details, such as access panels integrated into stepped ceiling patterns. The varied tastes of the senior partners also presented a design problem, resulting in a transitional scheme incorporating traditional elements (inlaid wood flooring, wood chair rails and wainscoting) as well as more contemporary ones (glass block, Herculite doors, and recessed incandescent lighting).

Right: The large conference room at its maximum size. Recessed acoustic wall dividers can split the room into two smaller areas.
Photography: Max Hilaire

Above: Looking from elevator lobby towards glass entrance doors and reception area.
Below: The conference room reserved for the law firm's senior partners.

55

Environetics Group

U. S. Life, one of the country's major insurance and investment companies, was previously housed on eight floors in Manhattan's downtown financial district. Having decided to keep only the corporate headquarters in Manhattan and to move the operations and policy planning groups out of the city, U. S. Life hired Environetics Group to help plan the move. The designers developed a program of needs with which the U. S. Life real estate department could work, and the subsequent search for space resulted in the choice of a 180,000-square-feet facility still in the planning stage and therefore able to accommodate the company's special architectural requirements. Among these were a full-service cafeteria seating 250, a data center, and an interior atrium. Private offices are very limited in number, with a consequent emphasis on conference and meeting rooms throughout.

Top of page: One of the conference areas located throughout the facility.
Above: Part of the employee cafeteria.
Right: Detail of glazed corner at conference area.
Photography:
Max Hilaire

Farrington Design Group

Atlanta, Georgia

404.261.6626

404.261.0798 (Fax)

http:/www.farrington.com

This Fortune 500 corporation's 170,000 square foot headquarters building is located at the gateway to downtown Atlanta and is the focal point of a triangular junction of two main thoroughfares.

The planning and design solution brought natural light and a sense of identity to the corporate headquarters. A careful analysis of the triangular floorplate of the office building determined that the majority of the enclosed offices be positioned along the perimeter of the space and around the typical support areas. A strong, classic identity was established on the executive level and specific design concepts are repeated on each floor. "Employee are delighted with the new building advantages", says Board Chaiman, Erwin Zaban.

A comprehensive environmental graphics program was developed to support the interior design concept and includes etched brass wall plaques for the executive level, acrylic plaques for lower floors, and exterior and parking deck signage.

Farrington Design Group

Premiere Technologies, Inc.
Headquarters Office
Atlanta, Georgia

Premiere Technologies, Inc. is an Atlanta-based telecommunications and software company founded to develop a new generation of telephony-based products, networks, and services. For the company's 16,000-square-foot headquarters, Farrington Design Group was asked to provide design appropriate for Premiere's youth and energy. The reception area, making a strong first impression, is bright with color -- gold, teal, black, and purple. The custom-designed receptionist's desk repeats the carpet's contrast of light and dark with surfaces of cherry and honey-stained maple. Beyond a panel of frosted glass, the conference room's table and matching credenza con-

Above, right:
Reception area, with view into conference room at left; corner of custom receptionist's desk is at right.
Right: *Executive office.*
Opposite: *Conference room.*
Photography: *Gary Knight*

tinue the theme of contrasting woods. In the executive office, where corner windows open to a panoramic view of Atlanta's Buckhead business district, a grouping of Le Corbusier armchairs in black leather create an "office within the office." Other facilities include a "World Link Room" for private internal meetings and, just outside it, a comfortable alcove for more impromptu meetings.

Farrington Design Group

Belleview Mido Golf Clubhouse
Clearwater, Florida

When Mido Development Company, Ltd., a Japan-based development firm, purchased the Belleview Mido Resort Hotel, they asked Farrington Design Group's help in constructing a new golf clubhouse for its 18-hole golf course. The challenge was to respect and complement the Victorian architecture of the nearly-100-year-old hotel, listed on the National Register of Historic Places and said to be the world's largest occupied wooden structure. Another factor was the incorporation of the color scheme (predominantly red, blue, and pink) found in Mido's golf clubhouses in Japan. The main lobby, tall enough to accommodate 20-foot-tall palms, is surrounded by a vinyl-clad colonnade, beyond which are a pro shop, restaurant, bar, kitchen, locker rooms, and management office.

Farrington Design Group

Civic Network Television
Washington, DC

Below: *Secretarial stations and a private office.*
Photography:
Eric Taylor

Civic Network Television (CNT), a non-profit distance training and video conferencing network, wanted a space that would reflect the creative, high-tech nature of its business. The space also needed to take advantage of the building's unusual triangular floor plan and column-free space, and, in addition, the designers were asked to work with the existing lighting installed between overhead beams. As Robert J. Shuman, President and CEO of CNT, assesses the result, "Farrington Design Group designed a space of curves and angles, open areas, and unusually shaped offices that are functional, comfortable, and full of subtle eye appeal." Total area is 5,500 square feet.

Earl R. Flansburgh + Associates, Inc.

77 North Washington Street
Boston
MA 02114
617.367.3970
617.720.7873 (Fax)
E-mail: erfa.com

Earl R. Flansburgh + Associates, Inc.

Donaldson, Lufkin & Jenrette
Boston, Massachusetts

Lacking the pleasures of exterior views, this regional office for an established investment company necessarily focuses inward. Its public areas employ traditional motifs and house a corporate collection of fine antique furniture, art, and accessories. The general office areas employ less formal motifs, concentrating on functionality and efficiency. Throughout both types of space, the use of medium-toned mahogany plays a unifying role and adds a feeling of warmth and stability. Faux finishes were carefully executed, and particular attention was given to the critical aspect of lighting. Total area was 23,000 square feet.

Above: Reception/waiting area.
Left: General work trading area.
Opposite, above: Small conference room.
Opposite, below: Large conference room.
Photographer: Steve Rosenthal

Earl R. Flansburgh + Associates, Inc.

Wellington Management
Headquarters
Boston, Massachusetts

The Flansburgh firm provided both programming and comprehensive interior design services for this 65,000-square-foot, three-floor corporate headquarters for a trust management firm. Each floor is organized into "neighborhoods," and small corner areas that serve as casual meeting areas for the staff. Long interior corridors are used as galleries for the firm's unique collection of contemporary art. A particularly challenging requirement was the design of the morning meeting room, which provides the firm with a forum-like atmosphere for employee participation and interaction. An open microphone system serves each position in three tiers of seats, and telephone and data links connect out-of-town offices as well. A center island contains controls for electronic slide interface, overhead projection, cordless microphone, audio recording,

and video cassette equipment, and three large interactive video screens are controlled by a signal processor. The end results are function served by technology and a feeling of being contemporary but not trendy.

Opposite: Contemporary art beyond row of trading desks.
Top of page: The morning meeting room.

Left: One of the casual meeting areas.
Above: Glass-walled, interconnecting conference rooms.
Photography: Hedrich Blessing

Earl R. Flansburgh + Associates, Inc.

The new Law Library at Boston College's Newton, Massachusetts, campus is the first phase of a four-phase replacement and expansion program of the BC Law School complex. The first of the building's three floors is linked to the existing law school building, and the first and second floors will be linked to future buildings. The symmetrical structure focuses on a central atrium dramatically crossed by a series of stairways. The library's 84,500 gross square feet include reading areas and carrel seating for 530 students, shelf space for 275,000 volumes, a 1,400-square-foot microfilm room, a rare books room, eight group study rooms, and administrative, technical and support facilities. The Flansburgh firm's design services also extended to site improvements: road relocation, grading revision, outdoor lighting, and landscaping.

Boston College Law School
Law Library
Newton, Massachusetts

Below: Reading and Lounge area with atrium beyond.
Opposite, above: Reading desk wired for computers.
Opposite, below: Stairs within the atrium.
Photography: Steve Rosenthal

Above and left: Two views of the Boston College Law Library's well-appointed rare books room.

Gensler...*Architecture, Design & Planning Worldwide*

Atlanta

Boston

Denver

Detroit

Hong Kong

Houston

London

Los Angeles

New York

Newport Beach

Parsippany, NJ

San Francisco

Tokyo

Washington, DC

Gensler

MasterCard International Purchase, New York

Gensler's work for the new world headquarters of MasterCard International began with the search for — and evaluation of — possible locations in and near Manhattan. The result of that process was the decision to acquire the 432,000-square-foot Nestle/IBM Building on 50 acres in rural Purchase, NY. Designed by I.M. Pei in 1983, the building offered large floor areas in three linked three-story pavilions, each with its own atrium and skylights. The decision promised potential savings of $250 million over the next 15 years. For the interiors, MasterCard's criteria were flexibility and synergy. To maximize flexible placement and employee interaction, Gensler devised a consistent, universal layout and a new standards program with a minimum of work station types and office sizes. Glass office fronts and work station panels only four feet high distribute light and views and encourage communication. Pei's original travertine and beige color palette was enhanced with Gensler's stronger additions of red and gold, reflecting

MasterCard's corporate identity. Selected manufacturers of private office furniture, conference room furniture, systems furniture, seating, and files participated in competitive bidding. In October, 1995, 700 MasterCard employees moved into the building, and, given the flexibility they needed, MasterCard anticipates the hiring of 400 to 500 more.

Right: *Atrium view of work areas.*
Below: *Glass-walled offices along curved corridor.*
Photography: *Peter Paige*

Left: *View into one of the MasterCard offices.*
Below, left: *Work stations and an informal conference area.*
Below, right: *Detail of the Gensler-designed graphics program.*

CONFERENCE ROOM
1W-B

1W
102

Gensler

Wachtell, Lipton, Rosen & Katz
New York, New York

For this prestigious law firm, Gensler was asked to provide comprehensive professional services. An initial building evaluation process led to six options, from which Wachtell selected 160,000 square feet on seven floors of the architecturally significant CBS Building. Initially, more space seemed to be required, but Gensler was able to devise a plan flexible enough to house some paralegals in future associate offices and to provide storage rooms convertible to other uses. In addition, all interior support space has been pre-wired for future private office space, and the major conference area holds reconfigurable tables and many seating options. As part of Gensler's space planning with Wachtell, the ratio of attorneys to secretaries was increased from 1.5 to 2.2, and the secretaries have been grouped in clusters of four. High priority was given to durability of architectural finishes and ease of maintenance.

Right: The firm's 8,000-square-foot law library.
Below: Detail of a private office.
Photography: Marco Lorenzetti, Hedrich Blessing

Opposite: *Large confer-*
ence room.

Right, above:
Secretarial work stations.
Below: *Two views of the*
stair and its glass para-
pets.

Gensler

Cushman & Wakefield
New York, New York

Below: *Gensler-designed stair spirals through three floors.*
Bottom of page: *Custom work stations for secretaries.*
Photography: *Marco Lorenzetti, Hedrich Blessing*

Also housed in Eero Saarinen's classic 1964 CBS Building are the offices of Cushman & Wakefield. Not in the business of owning or developing real estate, but rather in advising clients and managing assets, the client required secure advanced communication and data storage capabilities. And, in the expanding but unpredictable real estate field, flexibility was also crucial. The project's nine floors were divided into two levels of design: executive/broker floors with fine finishes, and support floors that interpret the same design details with less expensive materials. The boardroom, dominated by a custom-made table of black granite, is equipped with a computerized projection room, and a semi-public media area, filled with monitors, connects Cushman & Wakefield to its other offices around the world.

Gwathmey Siegel & Associates Architects, *llc*

475 Tenth Avenue
New York
NY 10018
212.947.1240
212.967.0890 (Fax)
www.gwathmey-siegel.com

Gwathmey Siegel & Associates Architects

"21" International Holdings, Inc.
New York, New York

In Mies van der Rohe's landmark Seagram Building, this 14,000-square-foot office houses "21" International Holdings, a multi-faceted investment company. Designing within that landmark has its pleasures, but also its prices, such as enforced retention of the perimeter's luminous ceiling, an inviolable elevator lobby, a restriction on placement of built-ins, and, of course, the building's pervasive grid. Gwathmey Siegel has worked respectfully within these limitations and, by means of such devices as a foot-high glass transom capping new interior walls, has made clear distinctions between Mies's design and their own. Within the facilities is a 3,000-square-foot Chairman's suite with reception, office, dining, and sitting rooms, furnished with early modern, Art Deco and Secessionist pieces. Materials throughout (maple paneling, integrally tinted plaster, beige marble floors, and cherry cabinetry) respond to the building's bronze window framing and form a quiet backdrop for the company's art collection.

Right: In a corridor, Yves Klein's blue Venus de Milo.
Below: Reception area.
Opposite, above: The Chairman's office.
Opposite, below: Secretarial station outside Chairman's office.
Photography: Durston Saylor

Gwathmey Siegel & Associates Architects

The Ronald S. Lauder Foundation Offices
New York, New York

The mandate here, according to Gwathmey & Siegel, was not to provide a "corporate image" for Ronald Lauder, an entrepreneur with wide-ranging investment interests, but rather to create a working environment that would complement the client's extensive collection of Secessionist furnishings and 20th-century German and Austrian expressionist paintings. The narrow shape of the 10,000-square-foot area also presented challenges in space utilization. Key to both aesthetic and functional solutions is a long corridor doubling as exhibition gallery, its simulated skylight alluding to the vaulted glass ceiling of Otto Wagner's famed Post Office Savings Bank in Vienna. Details throughout, such as custom work stations of ebonized cherry and Josef Hoffmann-designed carpet inset into cherry flooring, suggest (without imitating) the texture and articulation central to the craft ethic of the Secessionist style.

Above: Work stations seen from exhibition gallery.
Right: The office of Ronald Lauder.
Photography: Paul Warchol

Left: The central exhibition gallery.
Below: Main conference room.

Gwathmey Siegel & Associates Architects

The Capital Group
West Los Angeles, California

The Capital Group is a mutual equity fund management company based in West Los Angeles. For their 45,000-square-foot offices, they demanded a plan that would reflect their egalitarian belief that secretaries and support staff are as important to their success as are portfolio managers and analysts. Corner locations, therefore, are given to conference rooms, not private offices, and custom work stations, corridors, and offices share an integrated cabinet and millwork system of glass (some clear, some translucent) and maple panels. Rather than the typical desk-and-credenza arrangement, each office module has a small conference table for the discussions that are a key part of the company's investment approach and a U-shaped counter providing a generous horizontal work area. Because the company's "open door" policy created special acoustic requirements, recessed doorways are lined with perforated vinyl to reduce sound transmission, and ceiling and floor finishes provide additional noise control. Enjoyed by all employees as well as visitors is a double-height, clerestory-lit reception area spanned by a bridge that is a frequently used element of internal circulation.

Above: Corridor ceiling pattern reflects carpet design.
Below: The circulation bridge with floor of glass block.

Opposite: Reception area crossed by circulation bridge.
Photography: Tom Bonner

Left: Typical public corridor in the Capital Group installation.
Below: Custom work station designs by Gwathmey Siegel.
Bottom of page: Work stations and wall of private offices combine maple and clear and translucent glass.

Hellmuth, Obata & Kassabaum, P.C.
HOK Interiors

Atlanta

Berlin

Chicago

Dallas

Greenville, SC

Hong Kong

Houston

Kansas City

London

Los Angeles

Mexico City

New York

Orlando

San Francisco

Shanghai Rep. Office

St. Louis

Tampa

Tokyo

Warsaw

Washington DC

800.743.5507

HOK Interiors

Catellus Development Corporation
San Francisco, California

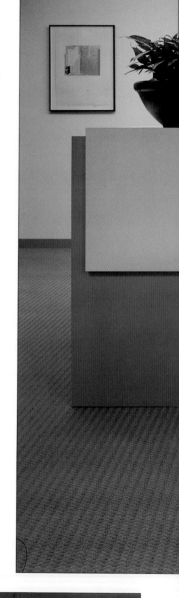

The floor area was irregularly shaped and the budget was limited, but the owner's new management team wanted its 60,000-square-foot headquarters to present a new corporate identity and to support the company's sense of direction and optimism. The HOK designers responded with a scheme utilizing modest materials, strong architectural forms and subtle colors. Two levels are connected by a new,

Above: *Double-height reception area.*
Right: *Stair railing intersecting column.*
Photography: *Marco Lorenzetti, Hedrich Blessing*

highly sculptural stair rising between existing beams, with bridges on those beams offering dramatic views and entrances to conference rooms. Sales and marketing solutions are aided by a series of rotating and stationary glass display panels, and promotional material is accommodated on tackable wall surfaces surrounding open and private meeting areas.

Above and left: *Two views of open-plan work areas.*

HOK Interiors

Meredith Corporation
New York, New York

The Meredith Corporation is a major publishing company whose magazines include *The Ladies' Home Journal* and *Better Homes and Gardens.* When it wanted to consolidate its four Manhattan offices in a single facility, HOK was chosen to provide architectural and interior design services for the 120,000-square-foot space. Open plan areas predominate, maximizing flexibility, and both open and closed areas are supplemented with video conferencing and multi-media presentation centers and a test kitchen. Colors are generally warm, and materials include marble, copper, glass, stainless steel, and encaustic paint.

Meredith's art collection, related to its interests in home and family, includes antique quilts and textiles, along with contemporary photography.

Left: President's office.
Opposite, below: Top of curving stair.

Below, left: Multimedia room.
Below: Entrance with reception area and stair beyond.
Photography: Paul Warchol

HOK Interiors

Above, left: *Assistant Vice-President's office.* **Above, right:** *Workstations.*

Below: *Anteroom.* **Photography:** *Paul Warchol*

Société Générale
New York, New York

With HOK's help, Société Générale, an international banking institution based in Paris, recently centralized their various New York offices. Because of a fast-track schedule demanding the highest level of participation and commitment, HOK established an ambitious schedule of consultations with the client's management: meetings with the CEO and the Deputy Managing Director occurred at least weekly, and meetings with the Chief Financial Officer occurred at least twice weekly.   Special features of the 325,000-square-foot offices include an executive dining room, an employee training center, a 3,500-square-foot data center, and a 25,000-square-foot, 225-position trading center.

HOK Interiors

Jones Day Reavis & Pogue Law Offices
Los Angeles, California

Below, left: Secretarial stations and entrance to conference room.
Below, right: A private office.
Bottom of page: Reception area.

Photography: Jon Miller, Hedrich Blessing

This national law firm relocated its West Coast regional office to larger quarters in a new 52-story tower. The elliptical forms used by HOK in walls and flooring patterns of the important public areas refer to the elliptical crown at the building's top. The relocation allowed the firm to enhance its function by increasing amenities, and among these are: various-sized case rooms; a reception/conference center with multiple audio-visual set-ups; a training facility; staff and attorney dining areas and kitchen; and increased capacity for library and central filing. HOK implemented a rigorous value engineering program to effectively control cost. By providing an overview of the available options and the initial and long-term costs associated with each choice at the onset, Jones Day Reavis and Pogue Law Offices was able to successfully realize the long-term goal of buying the most quality at the lowest cost.

HOK Interiors

HOK Alternative-Officing Laboratory
Houston, Texas

1. Harbor
2. Printer station
3. Touch Down
4. Fixed Address
5. Shared computer center
6. Group Address
7. Mission Control/production center
8. Conference
9. Audio conference center
10. Enclosed conference
11. Harbor

HOK Consulting has devised for itself innovative quarters utilizing a variety of "alternative-officing" methods. Based on intensive focus group discussions within the firm about the way groups work together and with clients, the design includes no private offices or assigned workstations. Instead, central "Group Address" areas provide flexible teamwork areas, with furniture that can be rearranged around flexible power and data ports, while corner "harbors" and an enclosed audio conferencing center accommodate more private telephone calls or teleconferencing sessions.

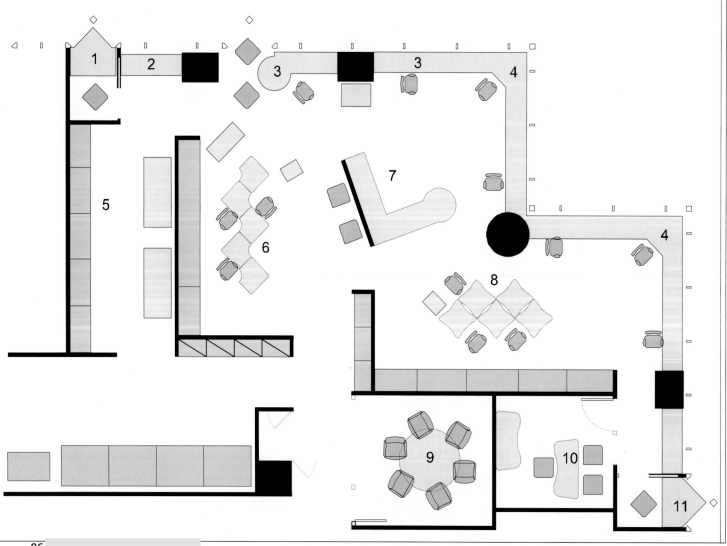

IA, Interior Architects Inc.

San Francisco

New York

Los Angeles

Washington, DC

Chicago

Dallas

Silicon Valley

London

IA, Interior Architects Inc.

Jack Morton Productions, Inc.
San Francisco, California

Jack Morton Productions is an innovative video production company for which IA has designed an appropriately innovative interior. Taking a 9,000-square-foot warehouse area as a raw beginning, IA has made it thoroughly functional, yet has retained its innate character, keeping its old factory window casings and emphasizing the overhead trusswork. Through custom glass enclosures, each office is visually open, responding to the client's wish for as much cooperative brainstorming as the design could encourage. New materials, such as scored panels of medium-density fiberboard and roughly finished concrete, complement the utilitarian structure, with pieces of pearwood cabinetry contributing more refined details.

Left, above: *Credenza detail in conference room.*
Left: *Corridor with exposed roof trusses above.*
Opposite, above: *The conference room.*
Opposite, below: *Two views of the reception area.*
Photography: *Beatriz Coll*

IA, Interior Architects Inc.

Bank of America
Domestic Private Banking Office
San Francisco, California

The design challenge in this 20,000-square-foot space was to consolidate three former banking facilities into one, to house most of the banking officers in systems workstations rather than private offices, to accommodate a wide range of banker/client meeting styles, and to maintain an image of elegance. Suitable display surfaces were also to be provided for the bank's extensive art collection, including works by Rauschenberg, Warhol, and Dine. The resultant color and materials palette is rich but subtle, comprising polished marble, blush maple woodwork, bead-blast stainless steel, woven leather wall panels, custom-designed carpet, and walls of integral-color plaster.

Above left: Doors from reception area have wood grids over glass panels.
Left: One of six private meeting rooms.

Opposite, above: Marble-floored reception area.
Opposite, below, left: Woven leather wall panels.
Opposite, below, right: Doorway framed in blush maple.
Photography: Beatriz Coll

IA, Interior Architects Inc.

The client wanted a "paperless" facility and wanted it quickly. Working on a fast-track schedule, IA carried the commission for an 80,000-square-foot banking operations center from initial programming through design, sitework, and construction in only eight months. This included conducting a series of "vision sessions" with the client's business and technical managers; from these were developed planning modules, column spacings, and adjacencies that seemed ideal for the client, and these in turn led to the configuration of the building shell. Literally, the project was designed "inside out." Because much of the center's work is done by temporarily assembled teams, work stations with maximum flexibility, as well as maximum space efficiency, were demanded. And because video conferencing is a cornerstone of the center's work, its reception area features a 10-foot by 20-foot bank of video monitors, used for company-wide broadcasts and image advertising. The center also includes a full-service cafeteria, health club, and staff "quiet room" lounges.

Bank of America
Auto Dealer Service Center
Las Vegas, Nevada

Below: Entrance to staff cafeteria.
Bottom of page, left: General office area.
Opposite and bottom of page, right: Two views of the reception/waiting area.
Photography: Beatriz Coll

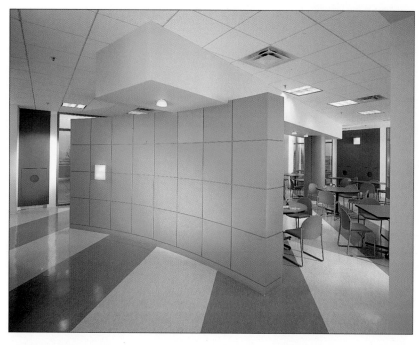

Above: Open-plan work area.
Right: Work station partitions vary in height.

Interior Space Inc.

1910 Pine
St. Louis, MO 63103
314.231.3838
314.231.9801 (Fax)

10590 Lincoln Trail
Fairview Heights
IL 62208
618.398.3800
618.398.4084 (Fax)

Interior Space Inc.

Blue Cross Blue Shield of Missouri
St. Louis, Missouri

Below: Four story atrium.
Opposite, above: Office of the Chief Executive Officer.
Opposite, below: Marketing presentation room.
Photography: Steve Hall, Hedrich Blessing.

In the heart of St. Louis, directly across the street from historic Union Station, an old electric utility building offered perfect quarters for the corporate headquarters of Blue Cross Blue Shield of Missouri. Its nine floors totalling 280,000 square feet was a comfortable fit for the 2,000-person work force, with room for such amenities as cafeteria and health center. To create a sense of unity throughout such a large space, ISI designed a four-story atrium which cuts into the building floors one through four.

The resulting open plan space is surrounded on all sides by color-coded carpets acting as circulation paths linking facilities on each floor.

One key to the job's success was the programming process, during which ISI's team of 11 architects and interior designers met weekly with members of the client's staff, discussing with representatives of every department their spatial needs and optimal proximities to other groups. An unusual outcome of that study was the decision to emphasize teamwork, openness, and accessibility, reducing the previous quotient of 200 private offices to only 12.

Interior Space Inc.

The Club
Kiel Center Arena
St. Louis, Missouri

Adjacent to -- and with thrilling views into -- St. Louis's new 20,000-seat Kiel Center Arena is a 17,000-square-foot dining and drinking establishment known as The Club. As designed by Interior Space, Inc., it has become, as intended, "the place to be." Although at some events its facilities are reserved for ticketholders for the arena's 85 suites and 1,600 club seats, its dining capacity for 400 is taxed nevertheless. At other events, the public is welcome to use The Club, and bar patronage can swell attendance to the allowed maximum occupancy of 2,000. Because the crush occurs always during the same couple of hours, solving circulation and crowd-han-

dling problems was one of ISI's paramount concerns. Sightlines to the action were another, and the various dining areas have been equipped with a complement of 54 television monitors that guarantee everyone a view.

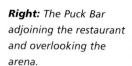

Right: The Puck Bar adjoining the restaurant and overlooking the arena.
Photography: Jon Miller, Hedrich Blessing

Interior Space Inc.

This 170,000-square-foot operations center was designed by ISI for a medium-sized Midwestern bank. Its functions are to process commercial and residential loans, checks, deposits, withdrawals, and account statements, and it consolidates more than 700 personnel who had previously been scattered in 15 separate locations. Circulation patterns in the two-story building focus on a central corridor with double-height skylit openings, providing a common reference point. Continuous open office areas hug the building's perimeter, their continuity allowing maximum flexibility in accommodating departmental contractions and expansions. Strong colors used throughout (termed "useful color" by ISI) provide directional aids and orientation cues. Major materials are painted drywall on metal studs, carpet, vinyl composition tile, suspended acoustic ceilings, and quarter-sliced birch veneer for doors and panels.

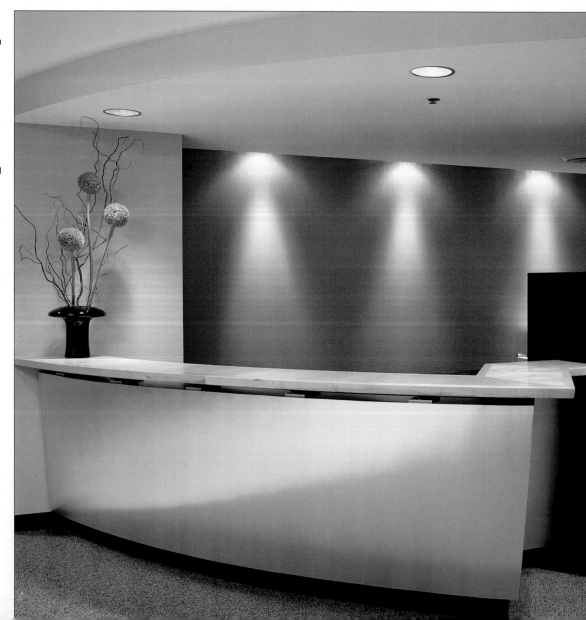

Right: A typical work station.
Below, left: Custom-designed reception desk.
Below, right: Corridor enlivened with color.
Photography: Alise O'Brien

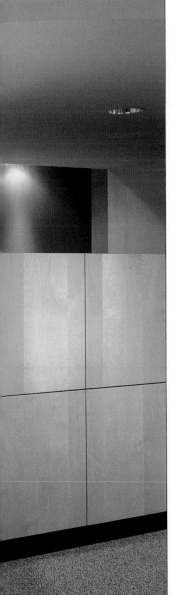

Interior Space Inc.

Interior Space Inc.
Own Offices
St. Louis, Missouri

Below, *left: The drafting room.*
Below, right: *An enfilade of colorful planes.*
Bottom of page, *left: Reception/waiting area.*

Bottom of page, *right: Conference room.*
Photography: *Steve Hall, Hedrich Blessing*

The offices designed by ISI for their own use are in an historic warehouse building (dating from the 1800s) in downtown St. Louis. The design is distinguished by its use of color, its respect for the old building's structure and character, and its recognition of a character split between the firm's "creative" studio and its "corporate' offices. The studio spaces are thus open in plan, with industrial lighting and with the original building materials exposed. The office spaces (reception area, conference room,

administration) have been given a more refined air with a finished ceiling, standard lighting fixtures, and a more subdued color palette; even here, however, imagination is much in evidence, with

painted drywall formed into dramatic slants and curves. Total area is 12,000 square feet.

Gary Lee & Partners

1743 Merchandise Mart
Chicago
IL 60654
312.644.1744
312.644.1745 (Fax)

Gary Lee & Partners

Newport News Incorporated
New York, New York

For the Merchandising, Advertising, and Marketing divisions of Newport News Inc., (a subsidiary of Spiegel Inc.,) Gary Lee & Partners have designed 45,000 square feet of office space, that will help accommodate anticipated growth over the next 15 years. In this specific office, housing 150 employees, the goal was to maintain an elegant corporate setting while also maintaining as flexible an infrastructure as possible. Key to achieving this double goal was the development by Gary Lee & Partners of a custom workstation design composed of interchangeable components. A variety of configurations of those components provides a

vocabulary of workstation types suitable for a large number of job functions.

Above, left: Circulation path doubles as display area.
Above: Lounge area in a private office.
Left: Reception/waiting area.
Photography: Marco Lorenzetti, Korab Hedrich Blessing

Gary Lee & Partners

Golder, Thoma, Cressey, Rauner, Inc.
Chicago, Illinois

On the 61st floor of Chicago's Sears Tower, with views to spare in three directions, are the new offices of the venture capital group Golder, Thoma, Cressey, Rauner, Inc. Gary Lee & Partners have provided understated interiors that bespeak quality with surfaces of mahogany and makore veneers, onyx and marble, and doors and panels wrapped in leather. An art program concentrates on contemporary southwestern painters and Native American artifacts. Perimeter offices share their light and views through glass partitions, their divisions aligning with those of the building's exterior. Work areas have been limited to only three types (the 15-by-20-ft. perimeter offices for partners, 10-by-15-ft. interior areas for associates, and 7.5-by-10-ft. stations for analysts and assistants), the result being great flexibility in forming and re-forming work teams. Total area is 17,600 square feet.

Left, above: Entrance with receptionist's desk at right.
Left, below: *Corridor between partners' and associates' offices.*
Opposite: *Perimeter office with glazed wall.*
Photography: *Jon Miller, Hedrich Blessing*

116

Gary Lee & Partners

Amerin Guaranty Corporation
Chicago, Illinois

Below: Work stations adjacent to the curved wall surrounding the support services.
Photography: Marco Lorenzetti, Korab Hedrich Blessing

Amerin, an innovator in the field of mortgage guaranty insurance, asked Gary Lee & Partners for interiors that would reinforce the egalitarian work ethic of their own business practices. Flexibility of space, ease of communication, and employee comfort were all to be provided. Clients and designers agreed that, to reach these goals, only two space standards would be used for the entire staff: a modest 150-square-foot enclosed office, and a 75-square-foot work station. The sense of hierarchy prevalent in most large corporations was thus replaced with collegiality. Elevators, fire stairs and other building core functions, along with auxiliary and support facilities such as copiers, files, and coffee bars, are all gathered within a sweeping oval wall, leaving the perimeter of the floor

free for the two work area types. Visual order, however, was imposed on the large open area by a 20-inch by 60-inch ceiling module and by a functional series of aluminum service spines between rows of work stations. Mies van der Rohe's furniture designs add a spirit of classic modernism and a suggestion of quality.

Right and below:
Two views of the typical work stations

Above: *Two spaces in Amerin's executive conference room suite.*
Left: *A vice-president's office.*

Lehman | Smith | Wiseman & Associates

1150 Eighteenth St., NW
Suite 350
Washington, DC
20036
202.466.5660
202.466.5069 (Fax)

Lehman | Smith | Wiseman & Associates

Houston Industries, Inc.
Houston, Texas

Below: *Executive conference room with lounge area.*
Photography: *Jon Miller, Hedrich Blessing*

Executive offices for Houston Industries have been designed by Lehman/Smith/Wiseman in a total of 40,000 square feet located on the top two floors of their new headquarters building at 1100 Milam. The two primary public functions, reception and boardroom,are centrally located and immediately adjacent to the elevator lobby. The more private functions, executive offices and the open areas incorporating the secretarial stations are situated on the periph-ery. Prominent finishes include Verde Giada and Statuary White marble, custom-designed hand-made carpet, silk fabric wall panels, and figured maple panels with pol-ished stainless steel inlay.

Left: *Secretarial station and office beyond.*
Above: *Boardroom ante-room.*
Below: *Private office.*

Lehman | Smith | Wiseman & Associates

The law firm of Howrey & Simon recently moved to the Warner Building on Washington's Pennsylvania Avenue. The building consists of the historic Warner Theater and a new office block designed by Pei Cobb Freed & Partners that is built over and around the theater renovation. Lehman/Smith/Wiseman has planned six floors of the building for Howrey & Simon attorneys, one floor (the building's second) for reception, a street-level entrance below that, and a below-grade floor for operations. Two other features are a sloping semi-transparent wall of glass and lacquer that circles the building's atrium and a 7,500-square-foot law library nestled between the dramatic structural trusses that span the width of the theater below. Lehman|Smith|Wiseman did more than the office design, however; the ongoing project has also included programming, building selection, base building modifications (such as street-level entrance) and preparation of tenant contract documents.

Above: Reception area.
Right: Circulation around building atrium.
Photography: Jon Miller, Hedrich Blessing

Above: *Law library between the building's structural trusses.*
Below: *Two areas with informal lounge seating.*

Lehman | Smith | Wiseman & Associates

AmSouth Bancorporation
Birmingham, Alabama

This financial institution's training and operating personnel, previously scattered in several downtown locations, have been consolidated in a 450,000-square-foot building on a wooded suburban site. The building's two towers are linked by a 12,000-square-foot glazed bridge, and it is on this bridge, with its expansive views, that the employee cafeteria has been located. Interior design responds to the idyllic location. Glass screens around work areas and walls of high-gloss plastic laminate trimmed with aluminum maintain a light, airy environment, complemented by dark terrazzo flooring. Accent colors of blue, red, and green designate the offices' different departments. At gathering points, such as conference rooms, the warm tones of pearwood are introduced, and pearwood appears again in the building entrance and in the credenzas and conference tables of the private offices. Leading to the cafeteria bridge, the servery is roofed with a custom ceiling aglow with light.

Top: *Training breakout area.*
Above: *Private office with small conference table.*

Right: *Employee cafeteria.*
Photography: *Jon Miller, Hedrich Blessing*

Above: AmSouth's work
stations, with lounge
area beyond.
Right: Cafeteria food
service area with custom
ceiling design by
Lehman/Smith/Wiseman.

Mancini•Duffy

New York, NY

Parsippany, NJ

Stamford, CT

Mancini•Duffy

Alliance for Downtown New York
New York, New York

Below: Reception/ waiting area.
Opposite, top: Work areas beneath ceiling plane.
Opposite, below: Conference room accommodating 20 board members.
Photography: Phillip Ennis

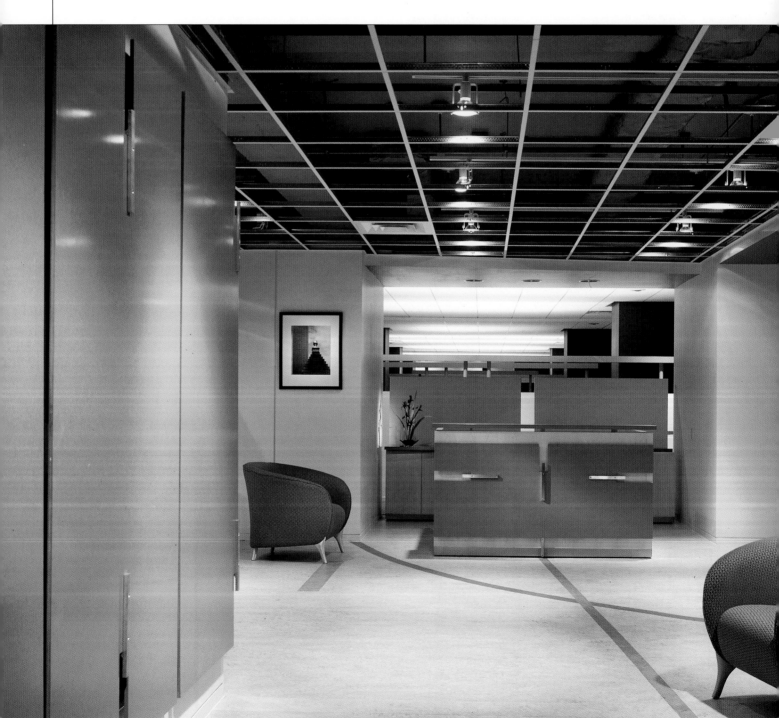

As a non-profit organiza-
tion and quasi-public
Agency, the Alliance for
Downtown New York (a
newly formed Business
Improvement District)
was very budget sensi-
tive. As a catalyst for
improving the down-
town Manhattan area,
the Alliance wanted to
develop its own 11,000
square foot quarters.
Demonstrating that
design excellence can be
achieved with limited
means, Mancini•Duffy
met both budget and
schedule. A pleasing
degree of openness pre-
vails, due to exposed
ceilings, neutral colors,
and spatial flow, with

geometric flooring pat-
terns adding visual dis-
tinction. Materials
include laminated safety
glass, natural maple, and
MDF (medium-density
fiberboard).

Mancini•Duffy

Witco Corporation
Greenwich, Connecticut

Witco, a "Fortune 500" company in the chemical manufacturing field, is the new occupant of an award-winning building originally designed in the 1960's. Mancini•Duffy had participated in choosing the building and wanted to maintain its integrity, but considerable work was needed to adapt its enormous 115,000-square-foot floors to today's more human-scaled workspace standards. Rather than linear stretches of identical stations, the designers provided a series of office groupings they characterize as "neighborhoods" and "townhouse clusters." At one end, the building was given a new granite-paved lobby area, and, democratically, the four valuable corner spaces were devoted to conference rooms. Witco's total area, including a terrace level cafe, is 285,000 square feet.

Left: The new lobby and reception area.
Opposite, below: Lounge furniture in waiting area.
Below: Work stations beneath the building's original lighting/cooling system.
Photography: Peter Paige

For its new 120,000-square-foot United States headquarters in New York, Daiwa Securities America, an international financial services institution, wanted both new American efficiency and traditional Japanese ceremony. Mancini• Duffy provided both, the former most evident in a 15,000-square-foot trading floor with all the requisite lighting, engineering and communications provisions, the latter most evident in the generous and well appointed areas for entertaining visitors. References to Japanese culture, such as screens -- some glazed, some paneled with damask -- are subtle, not overt, and motifs in the executive suites are carried through (but in less lavish materials) in the general office areas. A ten-foot ceiling height adds to the overall spacious feeling.

Opposite: Lounge area welcomes visiting guests.
Left: Reception area seen through glass screen.
Above: The trading floor.
Photography: Paul Warchol

Left: *Secretarial stations flank an impressive passage in Daiwa's executive suite.*

Mojo•Stumer Associates, P.C.

55 Bryant Avenue
Roslyn
NY 11576
516.625.3344
516.625.3418 (Fax)

Mojo•Stumer Associates, P.C.

Quality King Drug Distributors
Islip, New York

Projecting from the corner of a solidly monolithic 165,000-square-foot warehouse at a corporate park on Long Island is the much more lyrical form of a 15,000-square-foot wing designed by Mojo•Stumer for executive office space. While the straightforward warehouse form is built with concrete masonry units, the executive wing is a virtuoso display of aluminum panels, glass curtain wall, and glass block. Inside the offices, the glass block admits a plenitude of natural light, wall surfaces are softened with fabric-wrapped panels, and the curvaceous shapes of the exterior are recalled in the forms of desks and credenzas custom designed by Mojo•Stumer.

Above: *Executive office area projects from warehouse block.*
Right: *Custom designed desk in executive office with floor-to-ceiling glass.*
Photography: *Frank Zimmermann*

Opposite, above:
Fabric wall panels and
soft colors ameliorate
the building's industrial
character.
Opposite, below:
Shared executive office
with custom desks.
Above: Undulating
glass-block wall.
Right: Open plan office
area.

Mojo•Stumer Associates, P.C.

The Tilles Investment Company
Woodbury, New York

The Tilles Investment Company is one of Long Island's largest and most progressive real estate developers. Many of its clients are high-end corporate tenants who expect Tilles to be represented by an efficient, well-organized environment, corporate yet imaginative. Mojo•Stumer have provided just that, employing granite walls and flooring in the reception and executive areas. Elsewhere, walls of glass block and clerestory office windows insure a flow of light throughout the 5,000-square-foot quarters. Much of the interior furnishings is custom designed.

Opposite, above:
Reception area with custom-designed desk.
Opposite, below:
Waiting area with upholstered wall.
Below: Undulating wall of glass block.
Right: Granite-paved executive corridor.
Photography: Andrew Appell

Mojo•Stumer Associates, P.C.

Mojo•Stumer Associates Offices
Roslyn, New York

Below: *Entry/reception area.*
Bottom of page:
Drafting room with indirect lighting.
Photography:
Mark Samu

The first view from the building lobby into the open-ceilinged reception area of Mojo•Stumer's own offices is through a custom-designed wire-glass storefront. Its grid immediately establishes a sense of order, and the crisply detailed space projects the professional values and aesthetic concerns of the 45-person firm housed inside. Beyond the reception area, a gallery leads to a display wall with access to the open drafting rooms of the design, interior design, and production departments. Opening from a secondary circulation path are the firm's reference library, drawing storage area, and staff support facilities.

Juan Montoya Design Corporation

330 East 59 Street
2nd Floor
New York
NY 10022
212.421.2400
212.421.6240 (Fax)

Juan Montoya Design Corporation

Having designed a number of previous office/showroom areas and two residences for the same client, Juan Montoya was called on again for this 45,000-square-foot, two-floor installation in Manhattan's Garment District. Bringing together a number of previously scattered divisions and licensees, the new headquarters continues the palette of materials and colors that has identified Jones Apparel Group for more than a decade; among those are light oak woodwork, taupe walls and carpet, and polished chrome. Newly added to that palette are terrazzo floors, silver-leaf finishes, and metal-framed walls inset with clear and white glass. The two floors are linked by a private stair sculptured from flame-finish limestone, and throughout the showroom areas are furniture pieces custom designed by Montoya.

Right: Executive office with Montoya-designed furniture.
Opposite, above: Reception area with a collection of Italian glass vases.
Opposite, below: Another view of reception area.
Photography: Phillip H. Ennis

Left: *Jones Apparel Group executive office with glass space divider.*

Below: *Conference room.*

Bottom of page: *Waiting area in reception.*

Juan Montoya Design Corporation

Juan Montoya Design Corporation
Own Offices
New York, New York

Above: Montoya's own office. Guest chairs are a Montoya design; desk is Scandinavian. Beyond the trapezoidal wall at right is the conference room.
Right: Conference room.
Opposite: The ante-room, furnished with Louis XIII settee and Italian rococo library table.
Photography: Peter Vitale

The Montoya firm's own quarters, seen here, spreads expansively through the 10,000-square-foot top floor of a building in Manhattan's Chelsea district. Not quite a showroom, but definitely more than just an office, this is a space for entertaining clients, for dramatically displaying a few rare antiques, and for hinting at Montoya's taste and ability. First impressions are made in the elevator lobby, where battered walls have been troweled to a rough finish in shades of salmon and beige. From here, tall bronze and glass doors lead to the anteroom and antique-lined gallery, both given a floor pattern and black-and-white diamonds. Beyond are Montoya's private domain and two ample drafting rooms with custom-designed work stations. A full kitchen can produce meals or a cup of tea. Overall, a sense of luxe prevails, tempered by the direct and practical, such as overhead beams, pipes and ducts painted but left exposed.

Above: Elevator lobby with battered walls leading to Montoya's office.
Below: Drafting room.

ODI (C. O'Neil Designers, Inc.)

999 E. Touhy Avenue
Suite 350
Des Plaines
IL 60018
847.299.7700
847.299.7735 (Fax)

ODI (C. O'Neil Designers, Inc.)

Barco
Division of Marison Industries
Cary, Illinois

Barco, a manufacturer of rotary and swivel joints, recently relocated to a one-story build-to-suit facility comprising 7,000 square feet of office area and 18,000 square feet of warehouse. ODI, working with the building's architect and general contractor, provided Barco with an analysis of the company's existing furniture, a refurbishment program, and a limited program of new furniture procurement. ODI also provided space planning, installation coordination, and interior design, this last service including color schemes (incorporating Barco's corporate colors) and

Below: Conference room.
Right: Reception and waiting area with special ceiling treatment.
Photography: David Clifton

standards for finishes
throughout the building.
In the reception area,
ODI custom designed the
reception desk with spe-
cialty veneers and a
Corian top; behind it,
stepped partitions of
glass block transmit light
to the work stations

beyond and repeat the
form of the room's
stepped ceiling design.

ODI (C. O'Neil Designers, Inc.)

**Citizens Utilities Company of Illinois
Woodridge, Illinois**

ODI was contracted by Opus North Corporation, a design/build developer, to collaborate with them on interior finishes for the new quarters of Citizens Utilities Company of Illinois (CUCI), including a 25,000-square-foot warehouse and 27,000 square feet of office space. Working with the preliminary budget established by Opus and with the Opus specification manual, ODI researched finishes for the lobby, lunchroom, kitchen, assembly rooms, three conference rooms, library, plant meeting rooms, laboratory, restrooms, and general

Left: *The skylit research library used by the engineering department.*
Above: *An arc of computerized work stations in the utility control room.*
Photography: *David Clifton*

and executive offices. ODI and Opus met with CUCI personnel to determine the building's color scheme, developing it to include colors for laminates, tiles, wood, vinyl bases, and grout. Under a separate contract, ODI assisted CUCI with furniture assessment, specification, and procurement and also provided design details for custom interior features. During construction, the design team made field visits to assure that all work was in compliance with drawings and specifications.

ODI (C. O'Neil Designers, Inc.)

The offices for O+O, a developer of business and financial software packages, are non-traditional in many ways. Most striking of the departures in the modified "hoteling" concept used here is the absence of desks, for the company's programmers work at computers with keyboards placed in their laps. Leather-covered chairs from Arconas thus serve as work stations, and pods of four to six workers can be clustered at round tables that hold monitors. Because conventional desks, drawers, and files are all banished from the programming area, ODI equipped the employee break room with wooden lockers outfitted with shelves and drawers for supplies and personal belongings. In the equally radical reception area, known as the "greeting room," the usual receptionist's desk is also replaced with a comfortable chair, the company switchboard placed on its armrest, and guest chairs nearby can double as extra staff seating when needed. Custom lighting fixtures in office areas and greeting rooms are based on the O+O logo. Other work by ODI here included the design of private offices, a display room, a conference room, and a lunchroom.

158

Right: The production office area, where chairs serve as work stations.
Below: View into the O+O "greeting room."
Photography: David Clifton

Left: The O+O employee break room and locker room.
Below: A multi-functional conference room in ODI's installation for O+O.

The Phillips Janson Group

New York

London

Geenwich, CT

The Phillips Janson Group

Below: *Reception desk, with stair beyond.*
Bottom of page: *Conference room.*

Opposite, above: *Reception area.*
Opposite, below: *Work station cluster designed for collaboration.*
Photography: *T. Whitney Cox*

Money Magazine
New York, New York

Completed in 1992, this 50,000-square-foot installation in Manhattan's Time & Life Building was the last in a series of Phillips Janson projects for Time Warner and its subsidiaries, work that included restacking and retrofitting 650,000 square feet of the tower. The offices for Money Magazine differed from the other projects, however, because the magazine's Managing Editor wanted to eliminate most private offices and to organize editorial functions in a more open style where reporters, writers, and editors could easily collaborate. Phillips Janson responded with a system of "cadres," each composed of a cluster of four work stations and a central peninsula for group meetings. After several years of use, the magazine has reported great success with the design and its emphasis on teamwork.

The Phillips Janson Group

Bankers Trust Company
Command Center
Jersey City, New Jersey

This 8,500-square-foot computer command center runs and monitors all Bankers Trust's computer network and data storage equipment 24 hours a day, worldwide. Because the bank markets the center's capabilities to other institutions, the space itself was intended to serve as a marketing tool and has therefore been designed with visual theatricality. The center is approached through a sequence of dramatically lit spaces, and adjacent to it is a marketing/presentation room. Separating this room from the center itself is an angled wall of Liquid Crystal Diode glass that can be changed from clear to opaque by flipping an electric switch. Other related facilities are a reception area, an informal conference room, and robotics/storage units, and other materials include stainless steel and metalized plastic laminates.

Left: *The command center.*
Below, left: *View of the command center from the presentation room.*

Below, right: *Detail of custom-designed lighting fixture.*
Photography:
T. Whitney Cox

The Phillips Janson Group

Columbia House Company
New York, New York

Left: *Executive dining area beyond frosted glass panels.*
Below: *Luminous glass cube forms an entrance to the board room.*
Opposite: *Suspended steel stair.*
Photography:
T. Whitney Cox

Columbia House, a joint venture of SONY Music Entertainment, Inc., and The Warner Music Group, Inc., is the world's largest direct marketer of entertainment products (such as compact discs and video cassettes). Phillips Janson's work for the company began with a detailed space search and analyses of prospective locations, and the result was a move to 131,000 square feet in Rockefeller Center's McGraw-Hill Building. In these spaces, a predominantly neutral palette is enlivened with touches of bright color, such as circular red columns, and by the client's own art program. At the main reception area, a suspended steel stair connects the office's three levels; on two adjacent encaustic-painted walls, six video monitors play continuous loops of current music videos.

The Phillips Janson Group

Expanding an existing conference and training center in the same building, the Phillips Janson Group provided architectural, interior design, and contract administration services for the TIAA-CREF. A new reception/entertaining space on one floor and three new training rooms were connected with a sweeping stair of stainless steel and sandblasted glass panels to three additional training rooms on the floor above. The glass pattern complements the distinctive wall pattern of multi-toned woods. Training rooms are equipped with the latest in advanced audio-visual technology.

Above: Stair to upper floor.
Left: Wall detail.
Photography:
T. Whitney Cox

Perkins & Will

One Park Avenue
New York
NY 10016
212.251.7000
212.251.7111 (Fax)

Other Offices in:
Atlanta
Berlin
Charlotte
Chicago
Los Angeles
Miami
Minneapolis

Towers Perrin, a world-
wide management con-
sulting practice, commis-
sioned Perkins & Will to
design their newly con-
solidated New York
offices, two-and-a-half
floors totalling 100,000
square feet at 335
Madison Avenue. Two
related innovations in
planning are the "uni-
veral office" designed by
Perkins & Will in 110
square feet, with
telecommunications
hookups, specialized
task lighting and
ergonomic seating, and
the "hoteling" concept
of assigning these work-
spaces on a temporary,
as-needed basis, aided
by a concierge for taking
reservations.
Conference rooms and
workrooms are
equipped with tabletop
power and data ports,
and indirect lighting
throughout the comput-
er-dense environment
reduces glare.

Opposite: *Visitor waiting area.*
Below, left: *Stairway with part of the corporate art collection.*
Below, right: *Part of Perkins & Will's graphics identification program.*
Bottom of page, left: *Conference room.*
Bottom of page, right: *Teleconferencing facility with links to other Towers Perrin offices.*
Photography: *Marco Lorenzetti, Hedrich Belessing*

Perkins & Will

Towers Perrin
Parsippany, New Jersey

Towers Perrin turned to Perkins & Will again for the relocation of their New Jersey offices into 17,000 square feet of space in a Parsippany business park. Because the new office functions not only as employee workspace, but also as client information center, meeting rooms are equipped for client seminars and entertainment, incorporating the latest in multimedia technology, and part of the reception area can be partitioned off to serve the meeting rooms as a pre-function space. In these more public areas, cherry paneling and marble tiles lend a touch of luxury; in more functional areas, the same level of detail is achieved with more cost-effective materials, preserving a sense of continuity throughout.

Top of page: Cherry-paneled credenza in conference room.
Above: Visitors' waiting area.
Left: Open work area with private offices beyond.

Opposite: Office entrance.
Photography: Marco Lorenzetti, Hedrich Belessing

Perkins & Will
Iu & Lewis Design

Standard Chartered Bank
New York, New York

Standard Chartered Bank, based in London, has recently occupied two floors of office space in Lower Manhattan's World Trade Center. The design of the space is by Perkins & Will, working in collaboration with Iu & Lewis. Atypically, the design assigns the perimeter spaces, with their light and dramatic views, to open work station areas, their partitions kept low for maximum visibility. Private offices, with full-height glazing facing the open office areas, ring the building core. There is also a 60-person, 7,000-square-foot trading room, as well as spaces for operations, client services, marketing, and executive occupancy. Total occupied area on the two floors is 96,000 square feet.

Right, above: Stair with cantilevered treads leads from reception area to trading floor.
Right, below: A view of the trading floor and its carefully designed non-glare lighting.
Photography: Marco Lorenzetti, Hedrich Belessing

174

Above:
View into private office

Left: Looking from Standard Charter Bank's operations area.
Below, left: The employee lunchroom.
Below, right: Conference room.

176

Quantrell Mullins & Associates Inc

999 Peachtree Street NE
Suite 1710
Atlanta
GA 30309
404.874.6048
404.874.2026 (Fax)

Quantrell Mullins & Associates Inc

Smith, Gambrell & Russell
Atlanta, Georgia

Top: Stair in double-height reception area.
Below, left: Mahogany-paneled elevator lobby.
Below, right: Law library.

Opposite, top: Board room.
Opposite, below: Informal conference room.
Photography: Brian Robbins

To their design for one of Atlanta's most venerable and prominent law firms, the Atlanta-based firm of Quantrell Mullins brought something old and something new. The 70,000-square-foot office bows gracefully to tradition but accommodates the latest in technology. The most obvious traditional element is a double stair rising through a double-height reception area and, far from incidentally, conveniently linking the two floors of attorneys' offices. (A third floor, below these two, houses administrative areas, staff training rooms, and staff dining facilities.) Obvious, too, is a generous amount of mahogany paneling, stained a rich honey color, but its placement is rather unexpected: not in the partners' private offices, but rather in areas with more public visibility, such as the elevator lobby and the faces of secretarial stations lining the corridors.

On the more progressive side, vertical overhead storage above those same secretarial stations, built-in filing, and satellite file rooms and libraries (in addition to large, centralized ones) all promote efficient storage and retrieval of information. Quantrell Mullins's services to the client included an analysis of the firm's existing furnishings and a plan for the migration of pieces to be retained, custom rug and furnishings design, an art program, and a graphics program.

Quantrell Mullins & Associates Inc

If one had to summarize the Benckiser firm's interests in a single word, it might be cleanliness. Founded in the Rhine River industrial town of Ludwigshafen in 1823, the company has recently acquired 18 other companies in 11 countries, all producing household cleaning products, detergents, fragrances, cosmetics, water softeners, and the like. Retaining the venerable four-floor Benckiser family villa for executive offices and conferencing, the company has added a new three-floor building to houses the main reception lobby, administrative offices, support services, and a well-equipped conference center. Linking old and new wings is a glass-walled lounge and lucheon area that, with its view of courtyard gardens, is a major employee amenity. Total area is 40,000 square feet; total staff size is 85. An appropriately well-scrubbed aesthetic is achieved with a serene color palette that is predominantly white (including custom storage units, walls, marble floors, lacquered millwork, and most ceilings), given emphasis with gray and black (in carpeting, seating, and some casegoods), and further invigorated with accents of blue (as in the ceiling of the central circulation spine of the new build-ing and a coiling wall in the glazed link). The expanses of white not only connote cleanliness, but also help ameliorate a fundamental problem with the old villa: ceiling heights less than eight feet high. Other planning demands included designing and coordinating an open landscape office system and providing each work station, as mandated by both German law and Benckiser company policy, with an adjacent window.

Opposite, above and below: *Executive reception area in the existing villa.*

Below: *One of four executive offices.*
Photography: *Jens Willebrand, Foto Design*

Quantrell Mullins & Associates Inc

Ketchum Public Relations
Atlanta, Georgia

Below: Circular opening frames a work area.
Opposite, above: *Entrance*
Opposite, below: *Custom partitions separate work stations in a team cluster area.*
Photography: *Brian Robbins*

Designing offices for a public relations firm heightens the need for interior design that is itself a public relations tool. This 8,000-square-foot facility in Atlanta's First Union Plaza was no exception, but the tenant building allowance dictated a tight budget as well. Quantrell Mullins responded with virtuoso shaping and painting of gypsum board, plastic laminate, and other relatively inexpensive materials. New furnishings purchases were limited to files, seating, and movable pedestals for tables and desks. Most spaces share an overall openness, fluid with motion and color, the few enclosed areas including a conference room, equipped with the latest in audio visual technology, and a freestanding cylinder containing two small

areas for working in solitude and quiet. In the open areas, however, pivoting black-and-white-striped panels can be turned to create added privacy. In the reception area, the client's numerous awards are displayed in lighted frames and brightly painted niches.
Adjacent to the reception area, another advertisement of the client's capabilities is made by a tall millwork unit with video monitors and a shorter one with staging and filming equipment.

Left: *One of Quantrell Mullins's private offices for Ketchum.*
Below, left: *Conference room.*
Below, right: *Near the reception area, a video staging and filming area.*

RTKL Associates Inc.

Baltimore
Dallas
Washington
Los Angeles
Chicago
London
Tokyo
Hong Kong

1250 Connecticut Ave., NW
Washington
DC 20036
202.833.4400
202.887.5168 (Fax)
www.rtkl.com

RTKL Associates Inc.

Peabody & Brown
Washington, DC

RTKL worked closely with headquarters and local personnel in the selection and design of this Boston-based law firm's new Washington offices. After conducting two building test-fits, RTKL helped the client determine that moving, rather than renovating its existing space, would be the best solution to accommodate its growth to a 60-person office.

The new 26,000-square-foot space contains private and open offices, a reception area, conference rooms, library, central filing area, employee lunchroom, and service center.

RTKL's contemporary and sophisticated interior design is in keeping with office standards already in place in the Boston headquarters and Providence, Rhode Island, office.

A blue, khaki, and cream color scheme is carried out via blue lacquer accent walls, Swiss pearwood and Thai silk upholstered panels, and white marble flooring and countertops. Doors and furniture provide dark mahogany accents.

Right: Reception area with marble flooring and custom area rug.
Below: Conference rooms feature custom-designed tables and millwork.
Opposite, below, left: Upholstered chairs and silk wall panels in reception area. (Photo: Maxwell MacKenzie)
Opposite, below, right: View of receptionist's desk from elevator lobby. (Photo: Maxwell MacKenzie)
Photography: Scott McDonald/Hedrich-Blessing (except as noted)

RTKL Associates Inc.

National Football League
Players Incorporated
Washington, DC

Above: *The brushed metal of the reception desk marks a dramatic entrance to the office.*
Right: *Another part of the reception area takes its colors from the NFL logo.*
Photography: *Maxwell MacKenzie*

RTKL's design for the 7,000-square-foot licensing and marketing offices of the NFL Players Association fulfills the client's programmatic needs while imaginatively translating its new logo into three dimensions.

Since Players Inc. — the for-profit subsidiary of the NFL Players Association — receives and repackages large shipments of NFL-related merchandise, RTKL devoted most of the interior core to storage, assembly, and workroom areas. Private offices line the perimeter but allow natural light to penetrate the corridor.

The red, purple, and yellow of the association's logo are used as accent colors throughout the office. Curved lines becomes wall planes of color. The logo's square background is picked up in flooring, carpeting, wood paneling, and glass panels.

In the conference room, the football form surfaces in the elliptical shaped wall, the overhead lighting, and in a custom leather and English sycamore conference table (with black granite representing football lacing).

Right: *Private workstations are defined by a boldly colored wall plane.*
Below: *A double-sided merchandise display wall separates the conference room from the reception area.*

RTKL Associates Inc.

Embassy of Singapore
Washington, DC

For this 55,000-square-foot embassy at the gateway to Washington's new embassy district, RTKL performed a complete range of design services: architecture, engineering (structural, mechanical, electrical, and plumbing), interior design, and landscape architecture. The result expresses Singapore's image as both a growing, progressive country and a lush garden city.

The initial approach to the embassy is marked by a large garden, framed by two sides of the building and a garden wall. A diagonal stone wall divides the paved upper garden terrace, which is used for diplomatic receptions, from the lower, more informal perennial flower garden. Inside, a monumental stair leads from the entry level to the garden level below.

Right: *The reception area, overlooking an outdoor garden, is executed in granite, stainless steel, and etched glass.*
Below: *Frosted glass panels and wood frames evoke the character of Oriental screens.*
Photography: *Scott McDonald/Hedrich-Blessing*

The embassy's first two floors house consular services, dining, and public spaces; the administrative staff occupies the third floor. The ambassador's suite, offices for personal staff, and a library-meeting room are located on the top floor.

Colors and patterns representing the Republic's flora are applied to fabrics, custom carpets, and wall surfaces.

Above: *The library-meeting room features a lighting fixture custom designed by RTKL.* **Right:** *Glowing effects are produced by translucent panels behind wood grids.*

SCR Design Organization, Inc.

305 East 46th Street
New York
NY 10017
212.421.3500
212.832.8346 (Fax)
mail@scrdesign.com (E-mail)
www.scrdesign.com (Internet)

SCR Design Organization, Inc.

Republic National Bank
New York, New York

One of the most recent of more than 30 projects completed by SCR for Republic National Bank, this Investment Management and Trust Department occupies 22,000 square feet at 452 Fifth Avenue. While taking full advantage of contemporary materials and techniques, such as lacquered cabinetwork and generous areas of butt-jointed plate glass, the department creates a traditional atmosphere with the classical details of its interior architecture and furnishings. The project was constructed on a fast-track program.

Above: *Executive office.*
Right: *Controlled entrance to the department.*
Photography: *Mark Ross*

194

Above: Conference room.
Left: Column-lined general office corridor.

SCR Design Organization, Inc.

Meredith, Martin & Kaye
New York, New York

Meredith, Martin & Kaye (now retitled Robert R. Meredith & Company) is an investment advisory firm specializing in fixed income bonds for "high net worth" individuals. In keeping with the affluence of its clientele, the company wanted a working environment with an elegant residential aura. The entrance area sets the desired tone with marble flooring and mahogany paneling. In the reception lounge beyond, mahogany details continue, and the flooring becomes carpet overlaid with an Oriental kilim. The conference room, with touches of traditional wall molding, features comfortably upholstered seating. Total designed area was 9,000 square feet.

Left: *Reception lounge.*
Opposite, below: *Elevator lobby.*
Below: *Conference room.*
Photography: *Phillip H. Ennis*

SCR Design Organization, Inc.

BHF-Bank AG
New York, New York

Germany-based BHF-Bank A.G. wanted its New York headquarters to convey a prestigious presence and to project the German affinity for simplicity of design and excellence of engineering. The space chosen was 90,000 square feet on three floors of the former IBM Building at 590 Madison Avenue. SCR's design introduces an 18-inch-square module with the honed-finish marble pavers of the elevator lobby and reception area, a module continued with carpet squares in other areas and repeated by ceiling tiles. In the recption area, a wall of rough granite squares contrasts strikingly with an SCR-designed mural of multi-layered sandblasted glass panels. Other prominent materials are anigré wood

veneer and stainless steel trim. The conference room, divisible by a movable wall, epitomizes the goal of well-engineered elegance with anigré walls and a ceiling of metal pan acoustical tiles.

Right: Reception area.
Below: Elevator lobby of BHF-Bank.
Opposite, below: High-technology executive conference room.
Photography: Phillip H. Ennis

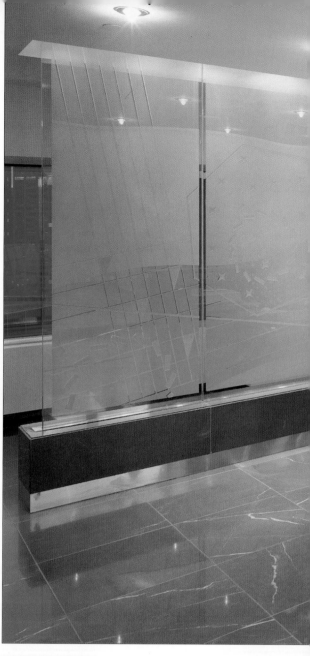

Left: *Executive office.*
Below: *Stair with wood-paneled parapets.*
Bottom left: *Trading/dealing room.*

200

Shelton Mindel & Associates

216 West 18th Street
New York
NY 10011
212.243.3939
212.727.7310 (Fax)

Shelton Mindel & Associates

On Manhattan's Madison Avenue, this is Shelton, Mindel's design for the 180,000-square-foot Polo/Ralph Lauren headquarters. It contains the offices of maestro Lauren himself and 400 others, as well as spaces for researching and designing new collections and almost two dozen showrooms for presenting those collections to buyers. Although all has been detailed with care, the traditional character of the most public spaces — mahogany paneling, Oriental rugs, potted palms — contrtasts strikingly with the lighter, fresher, more contemporary character of the actual offices and work areas. A standard ceiling height of just over eight feet has been altered by moving structure overhead ducts, plumbing, and power lines to allow generous uplighted ceiling coves, and, in some places,

Right: The stair to the sixth floor.
Below: Mannequins in the fifth-floor women's department.
Opposite: The reading room and resource center.
Photography: Dan Cornish

floors have been cut away entirely to create double-height spaces. Prominent materials include oak parquet flooring and blond maple for cabinetry and custom work stations, sisal for flooring in other areas, industrial glass-shaded pendant lighting fixtures, and stainless steel and glass wall sconces custom designed by Shelton, Mindel.

Left: *Polo/Ralph Lauren's sixth-floor library.*
Below: *The home furnishings plan desk.*

Shelton Mindel & Associates

Anne Klein Collections
New York, New York

The assignment in this case was more than the design of a single functional showroom within the Saks Fifth Avenue store in New York; it was the design of a prototype showroom that could be adapted for use in selected department stores internationally. In whatever location and in whatever configuration, the design needed to be strong enough to project a recognizable image, yet understated enough to serve as quiet backdrop to the clothing. Not an easy task. The specific site for the prototype was 2,000 square feet on Saks's second floor with an axial view of Rockefeller Center. Shelton, Mindel responded with a solution that has subtly but appropriately theatrical overtones, its elements recalling proscenium, wings, and backstage support areas. A canted ceiling plane is punched with square openings for incandescent fixtures,

and a hangbar system of nickel-plated steel, reminiscent of theater scaffolding, provides flexible display. In this carefully contived context, the clothing is the star.

Right and below: *Two views of the Anne Klein prototype showroom installation at Saks Fifth Avenue.*
Photography: *Dan Cornish*

Shelton Mindel & Associates

This single 20,000-square-foot office space at the intersection of Park Avenue and 57th Street, New York, had to accommodate a decidedly split personality, for part of the client's company deals in the lively world of venture capital, another part in the more conservative arena of investment banking. In designing the space, Shelton, Mindel were guided by a metaphorical model, comparing the venture capital sector with the bustling traffic and planted median of Upper Park Avenue, the banking sector with the quieter rectangularity of Lower Park Avenue. Throughout, gridded walls of clear and translucent glass make subtle reference to the curtain walls of office towers up and down the avenue. Most striking of all the components is a waving wall of green anigré wood, punctured by rectangular cutouts, that fronts the secretarial stations of the venture capital area and sits on a green and brown carpet. Its inspiration? The topiary of the Park Avenue median seen outside.

Opposite, above:
Passage in the invest-
ment banking branch of
the company.
Opposite, below:
Entrance and reception
area.
Above: Dramatically
curved wall in the ven-
ture capital section of
the office.
Photography: Dan
Cornish

Shelton Mindel & Associates

Fila USA, Inc.
Corporate Headquarters
Baltimore, Maryland

The computer-generated images shown here exemplify Shelton, Mindel's computer abilities, which also include three-dimensional animation and virtual walkthroughs of projected designs. The job shown, now nearing completion, is the U. S. headquarters for the Italy-based Fila corporation, an internationally prominent sportswear manufacturer. Its 100,000-square-foot area includes office, conference, and showroom spaces, all centered on a dramatic double-height atrium.

A stair to the upper level divides two canted walls faced with steel panels, creating a forced perspective effect, and the surrounding walls are given a glass-and-steel curtain wall treatment. The axial entrance into this expansive space will be through a dramatically restricted tubular corridor lighted with fluorescent strips.

Right: Shelton, Mindel's three-dimensional logo denotes Fila's international business.
Center and below: *In two computer images, views into the central atrium.*
Computer generated drawings: *Shelton, Mindel & Associates*

Silvester Tafuro Design, Inc.

50 Washington Street
South Norwalk
CT 06854
203.866.9221
203.838.2436 (Fax)

Silvester Tafuro Design, Inc.

Various installations at JFK International Airport, Jamaica, New York, and other airport locations

Silvester Tafuro Design, Inc. (STDI) aviation related experience covers a broad spectrum of project types and locations. At New York's JFK International Airport, STDI is currently undertaking extensive renovation and expansion projects at both the American Airlines and Delta Air Lines terminals. These projects encompass first class lounges, concession planning, concourse renovations, holdrooms and baggage claim areas among numerous other project types. Prominent among these installations are a First Class Lounge in JFK's Terminal 3 (seen at right) and a First & Business Class Lounge in Terminal 2 (overleaf), both designed for Delta Air Lines. The Terminal 3 facility incorporates a quite lounge, a television lounge, bar and restrooms in a 4,800-square-foot area. STDI designed the rectangular club with the illusion of being an ellipse by incorporating curved walls, a wooden elliptical shaped ring on the ceiling, and curved ceramic frit glass partitions dividing the space. Exotic finishes such as Block Mottle Makore (an exotic non-endangered wood species), Chinese slate and Brazilian granite were utilized throughout the club. They were utilized in unconventional applications as well as in high traffic circulation areas for their characteristics of being very durable and easy to maintain.

Right: Delta Air Lines's First Class Lounge at JFK's Terminal 3.
Below: Main lobby for American Airlines at JFK's Terminal 9.
Opposite, below: The Fenton Hill American Ltd. "America To Go" retail shop at JFK's British Airways Terminal.
Photography: Peter Paige (unless otherwise noted)

The Delta First & Business Class Lounge in Terminal 2 occupies a symmetrical area of 7,000 square feet. Business and First Class seating areas are kept separate, but they share a centrally located reception area, 17 telephone carrels with computer hook-ups, a bar area, restrooms, and four conference rooms. Ceramic frit glass partitions in each corner of the space and elsewhere define areas without visually enclosing them. The color palette is beige, camel, teal and aubergine, with teal as the chief accent in the Business Class and Public Areas, and with aubergine as the signature color in the First Class Lounge. Circulation areas are floored with beige limestone in a honed finish with gold-gray granite accents, furniture and lighting fixtures are trimmed with bronze and satin stainless steel.

Opposite above: Domestic check-in for Delta Air Lines, concourse level, JFK's Terminal 3.

Left: Hudson News at Houston Intercontinental Airport (Photography by Joe Robbins).

Above: Delta Air Lines' First & Business Class Lounge at JFK's Terminal 2.

Right: American Airlines' Admirals Club, JFK's Terminal 8.

Silvester Tafuro Design, Inc.

Below: The Delta Air Lines Satellite B-1 Hold Room at Newark International Airport.
Bottom of page: The Delta Air Lines Satellite B-1 gate area, Newark.

Photography: Peter Paige

Installations at Newark International Airport Newark, New Jersey

Since 1988, STDI has provided extensive interior design and project management services for major projects at Newark International Airport, working for both the Port Authority of New York and New Jersey and for individual carriers. Among this work has been the renovation of three of the airport's six satellites: first, for Delta Air Lines, a $6 million, 25,000-square-foot renovation of Satellite B-1; second, for American Airlines, a 25,000-square-foot addition to Terminal A; and third, extensive aesthetic upgrades for USAir in Satellite A-1. In addition, STDI is currently at work on extensive renovations of Terminal B's Satellites 2 and 3. Altogether, this work has encompassed concourses, ticket counters, gate areas, first class lounges, concessions, baggage claim areas, hold rooms, public rest rooms, jet bridges, flight services departments, and administrative offices.

Right: Telephone area, American Airlines Terminal, Newark International Airport.
Below: In Newark's Terminal A, the "Book Corner" retail shop for Hudson News.

Silvester Tafuro Design, Inc.

Below: Bar/lounge
area in the Admirals
Club designed by STDI.
Photography:
Peter Paige

American Airlines
Admirals Club
Newark International Airport

The 6,700 sf. American Airlines Admiral's Club at Newark International Airport was the third phase of the 25,000 sf. extensive renovation project to their terminal, connector, and satellite facilities undertaken by STDI. By using non-linear designs, placing the rooms at 45 degree angles, having a skylight running the entire length of the club and constructing a circular canted wall, STDI developed a sense of flow from room to room and diminished the "railroad car" of the 53' by 126' space. In order to create a warm comfortable atmosphere for weary travelers, STDI chose a color scheme which accomplished this without traditional wood paneling and fireplaces. The scheme included a blue and bronze palette for furniture, Anigre for architectural woodwork and a custom Zolatone for wall coverings.

Skidmore, Owings & Merrill LLP

220 East 42nd Street
New York
NY 10017
212.309.9500
212.309.9750 (Fax)

224 South Michigan Ave.
Chicago
IL 60604
312.554.9090
312.360.4545 (Fax)

333 Bush Street
San Francisco
CA 94104
415.981.1555
415.398.3214 (Fax)

1201 Pennsylvania Ave. NW
Washington, DC
20004
202.393.1400
202.662.2323 (Fax)

46 Berkeley Street
London W1X 5FP
United Kingdom
0171.930.9711
0171.930.9108 (Fax)

Skidmore, Owings & Merrill LLP

Chase Manhattan Bank Trading Facility
New York, New York

Having designed the Lower Manhattan landmark building at One Chase Manhattan Plaza back in 1960, SOM (Skidmore, Owings & Merrill LLP) returned recently to insert new trading facilities into the tower. Two trading floors needed to accommodate 228 traders each, with all their requirements of space, computers, power, glare-free lighting, and the dissipation of generated heat, and infrastructure was also provided for the future addition of a third floor with another 228 positions. New generators were added on the tower's roof, served by new tanks and fuel lines, and the trading rooms were provided with Uninterrupted Power Supply, chilled water

lines, cabling risers, and a new data center. A less technical -- but equally important -- requirement for such large areas was the maximizing of ceiling height, a problem made more difficult by the need for six-inch-high raised floors for the grids of cable routes. SOM achieved a new clear height of ten feet by removing the existing mechanical systems overhead and locating new fan coil units at the building's perimeter and core. In addition to the trading floors are associated amenities: offices, video conferencing areas, copy centers, coat rooms, and food service facilities. The materials palette, sympathetic to the original structure, includes stone, stainless steel, cherry

Above: One of the two trading floors.
Right: Stone and steel connecting stair.

Opposite, above: Reception desk, seating, and stair.
Opposite, below: Food service area.
Photography: Jon Miller, Hedrich Blessing

paneling, and, on core enclosures, a highly durable polyester resin finish. A spiral stair of stone and steel connects the project's three levels. Total designed area is 73,200 square feet.

Skidmore, Owings & Merrill LLP

Financial Institution
New York, New York

Occupying a total of 50,000 square feet on two high floors of New York's Citicorp building, these offices for a rapidly growing investment firm demanded the utmost in flexibility. Working with the established grids of the building's structure, glazing, and ceiling modules, the SOM designers have responded with a universal lighting plan and a system of demountable partitions. Office enclosures that are largely of clear glass and doors of both clear and etched glass give most work areas a sense of openness and a share of the unparalled views. The motivated staff works long hours in this environment, but their work is rewarded by — and their work spaces supplemented by — a number of on-site amenities: food service facilities offering breakfast-through-dinnertime food, meeting rooms both formal and casual, a library and magazine room, and a fitness center with changing rooms, lockers, and showers for men and women.

Far left: View from reception area to gallery and dining room beyond.
Above: The library for the firm's senior executives.
Photography: Marco Lorenzetti, Korab Hedrich Blessing

Above: View from reception area to board room.

Above, right: Near trading room and a lounge area, a low partition shields food service area.

Below: Board room is furnished with more A/V technology than meets the eye, such as microphones in the custom lighting fixtures.

Opposite: Glazed wall of a typical office lets others share the Manhattan view.

Skidmore, Owings & Merrill LLP

Kirkland & Ellis
New York, New York

Left: *Reception area under a metal grid.* **Below:** *The double-height library and its glass stair.* **Photography:** *Michael Moran*

The planning module is a frequently employed tool for bringing order and cohesion to today's corporate interiors, but seldom has it been used more pervasively or more persuasively than in the two-floor, 48,000-square-foot Manhattan offices for the law firm of Kirkland and Ellis. The resultant order is joined by a liberating sense of openness and light, with perimeter offices largely enclosed in glass. Where privacy was wanted for lawyers' offices, a pearlescent glass layer was laminated between two ribbed layers, blocking the view but still transmitting the light. The heart of the office is a two-story law library, featuring a dramatic stair that, with open risers and laminated glass treads, continues the theme of lightness.

Howard Snoweiss Design Group

4200 Aurora Street
Coral Gables
FL 33146
305.461.3131
305.461.3330 (Fax)

Howard Snoweiss Design Group

Fowler, White, Burnett, Hurley, Banick, Strickroot, P.A.
Miami, Florida

In 1994, learning that their building had been sold, this Miami law firm came to Howard Snoweiss Design Group to develop the concept for their new space. Project designer Jim O'Shaughnessy, who had previously designed their space in 1988, was again assigned that complex task.

The new space was not to be more of the same design, but was to be based on a through reassessment of the firm's work flow and space requirements. Detailed interviews with key individuals from all disciplines of the firm led the designers to a novel dual-corridor system, one corridor flowing between the bank of lawyers' offices and the secretarial groupings, and the more internal corridor giving access to the paralegal groupings and accom-modating filing and printer stations. This organization has proved to provide a minimum of cross-traffic and a rare degree of sound control. ADA guidelines for accessibility, not only for restrooms but for work stations as well, were also an important design determinant. The net result was that the former office of 52,000 square feet, based on assumptions of the '80s, was recon-sidered for the '90s and made totally functional in 41,000 square feet.

Right: The law firm's reception and waiting area.
Photography: Nancy Robinson Watson

Left: Work station and curving circulation path.
Left, below: Another seating group in the reception area.
Below: Conference room.
Opposite: View from reception area into conference room.

Howard Snoweiss Design Group Ernst & Young
Miami, Florida

Two pairs of seemingly irreconcilable conflicts faced the designers here. The client, a major national accounting firm, was strongly attracted to the vacant 39th floor of Miami's First Union Fianancial Center, formerly the executive headquarters of Southeast Bank, loving its spectacular views and its 10-foot ceiling height, but definitely not loving its expansive layout and expensive contemporary detailing, both examples of '80s opulence. The other conflict was that they wanted a conservative, traditional look with elegant finishes, but wanted it within the building's construction allowance of $32 per square foot. The Howard Snoweiss Design

230

group resolved both con-
flicts, devising a series of
details that could be
combined with the exist-
ing contemporary ele-
ments to produce a
warmer, more comfort-
able effect. Wood trim,
for example, combining
mahogany and cherry,
was used in conjunction
with existing granite
walls; honed granite
floors were partly cov-
ered with custom-
designed area rugs and
antique Orientals; the
teak files that were left

by the previous tenant
were incorporated into
the plan; and executive
offices were modified to
accommodate new doors
and new types of light-
ing. At the end of the
process, the new envi-
ronment was just what
Ernst & Young had in
mind; so was the cost.

Above: *Visitors' waiting
area with Oriental rug.*

Spillis Candela & Partners, Inc.

Corporate Headquarters:
800 Douglas Entrance
Coral Gables
FL 33134
305.444.4691
305.447.3576 (Fax)

Regional Offices:
200 S. Orange Avenue
Suite 1240
Orlando, FL 32801
407.422.4220
407.423.4692 (Fax)

1720 Eye Street, NW
Suite 500
Washington, DC
20006
202.785.8550
202.728.4054 (Fax)

Spillis Candela & Partners, Inc.

Financial Institution
Jacksonville, Florida

Above: Platform area of banking hall.
Right, above: President's office.
Right, below: Executive waiting area.

Opposite, above: Entrance/reception area
Opposite, below: Teller area of banking hall.
Photography: Dan Forer

This headquarters for a financial institution occupies 42,000 square feet in downtown Jacksonville. One component is a branch bank with 15 teller positions, occupying approximately a third of its building's ground floor lobby area; the bank also has a safety deposit vault and custom-designed work stations for the customer service representatives. On two floors of the building above, the other component is executive office space, including a suite for the Chief Executive Officer and a reception area with vaulted ceiling and wood paneling with inlaid accent stripes. Spillis Candela provided a complete range of services, both architectural design and interior design.

Spillis Candela & Partners, Inc.

International Generating Company
Latin America Division
Coral Gables, Florida

With its headquarters in Boston, International Generating Company (or, more familiarly, InterGen) is a global power company dedicated to the development and management of electric generation facilities. These new 7,500-square-foot South Florida offices, completed in 1995, serve the company's interests in Mexico, the Caribbean, Central America, and South America. Mandated to create a contemporary environment on a modest budget, Spillis Candela used the selective application of strong, saturated paint colors to achieve design impact and to reinforce the organization of the interior space. Materials are simple, finishes inexpensive, and, appropriate to the client's business. Lighting fixtures are given an unusually prominent place in the design scheme.

Above: *Secretarial stations.*
Left: *Reception area.*
Right: *Executive office.*
Photography: *Nancy Robinson Watson*

Spillis Candela & Partners, Inc.

USAA
Southeast Regional Home Office
Tampa, Florida

Above: Waiting area
and glass-fronted offices.
Right: Main lobby with
receptionist's desk and
stair.
Photography: Nick
Merrick, Hedrich Blessing

This large (520,000-square-foot) facility houses the southeast regional home office for USAA, a worldwide insurance and financial services association serving almost three million customers (primarily members of the U.S. military and their families). The facility's appropriately large-scale reception area is double height, with a stair dramatically cantilevered from a curving wall of wood paneling. A circular inset of custom-designed wool carpet creates a seating island in the terrazzo flooring. Throughout the general office areas, the drama continues but is achieved with simpler and more economical means, most notably brightly painted accent planes of drywall dividing the work areas. At the entrance and servery of the employee cafeteria, sculpturally curved forms reappear, surfaced with colorful but durable glass mosaic.

Left: Open work area with turquoise accent wall.
Below: Serving area of cafeteria.

Staffelbach Designs and Associates Inc

2525 Carlisle

Dallas

TX 75201

214.747.2511

214.855.5316 (Fax)

104520,2740@compuserve.com

Staffelbach Designs and Associates Inc

Price Waterhouse
Dallas, Texas

The Staffelbach design for Price Waterhouse supports that client's plans to relocate their offices, transform their image, and reconfigure their conventional office layouts into a "hoteling" environment. Such a concept of work units without permanent assignment was deemed ideal for employees who are often out of the office working with their clients. Planning such a radical change required careful preparation,

however; the program-
ming process occurred in
various stages over a
two-year period, and
focus group sessions
staged by the designers
included representatives
at every level of the
client's staff. Finally,
clear criteria for the
planning of the space
emerged. These have
been made manifest in a
design of soft neutral
colors, emphasizing
brightness and light, and
using materials and fin-
ishes appropriate for
such a concept and its
consequent high traffic
and heavy usage.

**Above; opposite,
above; and opposite,
below, left:** *Three views
of the reception area.*
**Opposite, below,
right:** *Furniture/art
grouping outside confer-
ence room.*
Below: *View from circulation area into an
office.*

Photography: *Paul
Bardagjy, Through the
Lens*

Staffelbach Designs and Associates Inc

Sterling Software
Las Colinas, Texas

Sterling Software is a leading software company and now a part of Sterling Commerce. Relocating their headquarters to a highrise in the Las Colinas business development outside Dallas, they asked the Staffelbach firm to create for them a clean, sophisticated image. Both management and employees emphasized the need to manage workspace clutter, to keep offices organized, to foster interaction among work teams, and to generally improve the quality of their work environment. Management added the challenge of bringing

art into that environment. The design team responded with interiors of harmony and calm, designing customized millwork and giving special attention to the balancing of reflective and non-reflective surfaces.

Opposite: Two views of the reception area.
Left: Conference room.
Below, left: Glass-walled monitor area.
Below, right: Employee break room.
Photography: Paul Bardagjy, Through the Lens

Staffelbach Designs and Associates Inc

**GTE Telephone Operations
World Headquarters
Hidden Ridge, Texas**

Left: Board room.
Above, right: Work station in general office area.
Right: Corridor leading to stairway.

Photography: Jon Miller, Hedrich Blessing

In the unlikely location of gently rolling mesquite prairie outside Dallas, the Staffelbach firm has designed more than a million square feet of world-class office space. Housing almost 3,000 members of GTE's telecommunications staff, the facility is reportedly the result of the largest corporate consolidation in American business history. The multiple missions of the project were to respond to the surrounding natural landscape, to respond as well to the needs and desires of the workers, to stimulate their leaders, and to manifest the highest of high-tech office technologies. Helping accomplish this last mission are many of the client's own products: satellite broadcast and integrated networks, fiber optics carrying both voice and data, and closed circuit television.

Above: *Executive reception area.*

Below, left: *Waiting area and secretarial stations near executive offices.*

Below, right: *The on-site gymnasium.*

Swanke Hayden Connell Architects

295 Lafayette Stleet
New York
NY 10012
212.226.9696
212.219.0059 (Fax)
*@shca.com (E-mail)

One Thomas Circle, NW
Suite 580
Washington, D.C. 20005
202.785.3331
202.785.3902 (Fax)
*@dc.shca.com (E-mail)

First Union Financial Center
200 South Biscayne Blvd.
Suite 970
Miami, Florida 33131-2300
305.536.8600
305.536.8610 (Fax)
*@miami.shca.com(E-mail)

12A Finsbury Square
London, England
EC2A 1AS
44171.374.4371
44171.374.0506 (Fax)
*@london.shca.com (E-mail)

Mithat Ulu Unlu Sok.
No: 21, D8
Zincirlikuyu, Istanbul
Turkiye 80300
90.212.212.2420
90.212.212.2328 (Fax)
*@istambul.shca.com (E-mail)

Swanke Hayden Connell Architects

Bertelsmann, Inc.
New York, New York

Above: *Entrance area with front desk.*
Left and opposite: *Two views of the electronics-equipped boardroom and its custom triangular table representing the corporate logo of BMG.*
Photography: *Peter Paige*

Bertelsmann is an international publishing giant whose subsidiaries include Bantam Doubleday Dell and the music companies RCA, BMG, and BMG Direct Marketing. For this company, Swanke Hayden Connell has designed 720,000 square feet of headquarters facility in the Bertelsmann- owned tower at 1540 Broadway, overlooking Times Square. It is the first time that the corporation's varied elements have been assembled at one location. The nature of the company's business dictated a plan that is 55 percent private office space; in addition, there are open work areas, a computer facility, conference and audio-visual presentation rooms, recordings archives, cafeteria, coffee bar, tape mastering studios, and main lobby reception area. The complex programming process began in 1990, site selection in 1992, and job completion was in 1993.

Opposite, above:
Office of the
chairman.
Opposite, below:
Open plan work area.
Right: Employee
coffee bar.
Below: An executive
dining area.

Swanke Hayden Connell Architects

Above: *Custom-designed reception desk.*
Opposite: *Open-plan work area under vaulted ceiling.*
Photography: *Jeremy Cockayne*

Embankment Place is a unique, large-floored building suspended above (and using the air rights of) London's historic Charing Cross railway station. Here Swanke Hayden Connell have designed 350,000 square feet for the international accounting firm of Coopers & Lybrand. Supporting the cellular and open-plan office areas are service centers, copying rooms, vending areas, equipment rooms, client and staff dining and meeting suites, and related kitchen, reception, and ancillary areas. SHC also refined workstation standards to create a flexible, modular space planning unit. SHC's brief included preparation of schematic and detailed designs and, in liaison with the client's construction manager, construction documentation and implementation.

Left: Coopers & Lybrand's cafeteria and dining area, as designed by Swanke Hayden Connell.
Below: View of atrium art gallery.

The Switzer Group. Inc.

535 Fifth Avenue
New York
NY 10017
212.922.1313
212.922.9825 (Fax)

The Switzer Group, Inc.

Integrated Resources, Inc.
New York, New York

Working on a fast-track schedule that allowed personnel relocation to begin one year from the inception of the project, The Switzer Group designed a 450,000-square-foot facility supporting the activities of 1,300 employees. Ongoing reorganization and the tight schedule demanded adjustments in the field, and the necessary versatitlity was aided by systems furniture workstations (by Herman Miller) and by offices powered through raised floors. The installation included an expansive atrium/lobby, a brokerage/trading facility, a 20,000-square-foot data center, cafeteria, lounge, multi-purpose conference rooms, medical center and fitness center. The Switzer Group also arranged dual substation power provision, and designed a UPS/generator system and a 250-ton cooling system.

Opposite: Corridor and reception desk.
Left: Executive board room.
Below: Atrium dining facility.
Photography: Mark Ross

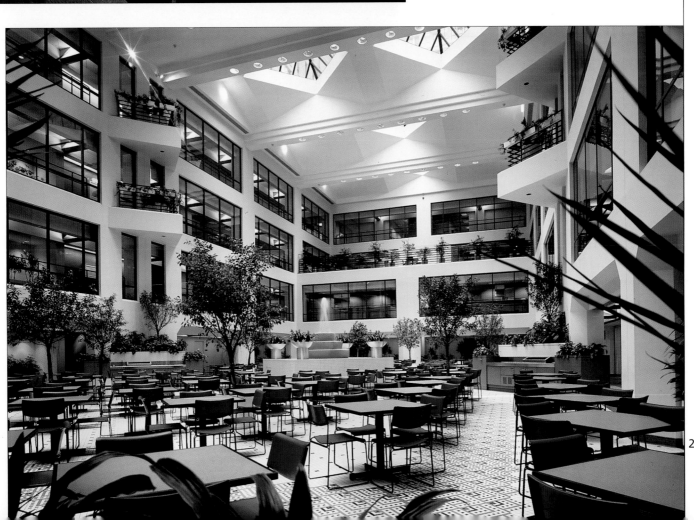

259

The Switzer Group, Inc.

Group W
Westinghouse Broadcasting Corporation
New York, New York

For the relocation of Westinghouse Broadcasting's corporate headquarters into 42,000 square feet of Manhattan office space enjoying exceptional city views, the design brief was to provide the highest of quality within a transitional style, the latest in technology easily accessible but not readily apparent. Inherent problems to be overcome were low ceiling heights, an enormous building core, and, encircling the core, necessarily long corridors. Facilities to be housed were largely for executives and sales department personnel. Secretarial stations are custom designed in wood, the reception desk combines green marble with figured anigré wood, and the executive board room has been provided with a very sophisticated audio-visual wall with synchronized lighting, front projection, and television monitors for displaying the programs of all Westinghouse's station affiliates.

Above, right: *View into executive boardroom.*
Right: *Main reception waiting area with antique Oriental screen.*
Opposite, above: *Elevator lobby.*
Opposite, below: *Marble reception desk and main corridor.*
Photography: *Paul Warchol*

The Switzer Group, Inc.

EMI Music Worldwide
New York, New York

The Switzer Group helped EMI Music Worldwide relocate to three small contiguous floors totaling 27,000 square feet. An elegant yet contemporary and progressive image was wanted, and the designers responded with an impressively scaled and detailed reception/waiting area featuring leather seating and a custom-designed receptionist's desk of brushed aluminum. Adjoining the reception area is a grand stair connecting the three levels and, behind the stair, a three-story-high abstract color mural. Carpet designs are also custom. Aggregate marble panels, composed of marble chips set in resin, are outlined in brass and used as accent flooring and wall covering. Figured wood paneling and stainless steel are also prominent in the materials palette.

Opposite, above:
Entrance lobby.
Opposite, below:
Reception area with
brushed aluminum desk.
Above: Horseshoe-
shaped stair connects
EMI's three levels.

Photography: Durston
Saylor

The Switzer Group, Inc.

Consolidated Edison Company of New York
Staten Island, New York

As part of the giant New York utility company's Customer Service Program, The Switzer Group has helped upgrade its community "business offices" into "customer service centers." Prototypes for these have been designed for the Jamaica, Brownsville, and Staten Island areas of New York, their sizes ranging from 3,000 to 20,000 square feet each. One of the smallest, seen here, is Con Edison's Davis Avenue center, occupying an existing brick structure that was gutted, structurally modified, and given a new entrance pavilion of glass block and pigment-ed stucco. Its facilities include areas for a receptionist, tellers' stations (one of them dedicated to disabled customers), customer service representatives, field representatives, a cashier, a manager, employee lounge and lockers, and support equipment. Facade renovation was also provided, as was the design of parking areas and security-related elements.

Above: Entry pavilion faced with glass block.
Right: The utility's public transaction area, designed by The Switzer Group.
Photography: Durston Saylor

TAS Design

145 Hudson Street
New York
NY 10013
212.334.8319
212.334.8025 (Fax)

TAS Design

Sony Music International Miami, Florida

New offices for Sony Music International, Latin America, have been skillfully inserted into the top two floors of a 1936 building in Miami's South Beach area. The 20,000-square-foot space, however, displays none of the usual Art Deco mannerisms, but is instead characterized by light, air and openness. The top level's almost-15-foot ceiling height has given TAS Design ample opportunity for manipulating space in unusual ways,

Above: Stair joining the two levels has stone treads, steel stringers, and aluminum rails.
Left: A curved wall of cherry backs the reception desk. (Photo by Nancy Watson)
Opposite: Looking from glass-walled office to reception desk.
Photography: Paul Warchol, unless otherwise noted

such as the curved inser-
tion, at the 10-ft. level,
of umbrella-like disks
that, without enclosure,
mark important turning
points in the circulation
pattern below. Above
these and other inserted
layers, the building's
rough concrete slabs and
beams have been left
exposed. Curved storage
walls, faced with cherry,
also define special areas
without confining them.
Two conference rooms,
one on each floor, share
views of the adjacent
metal and masonry stair
(and light from the sky-
light above it) through a
double-height wall

designed as a cascade of
translucent panels of
laminated glass.
Appropriately for its
tropical context, Sansone
describes the wall as
"the biggest jalousie
window ever."

Above: Through a cus-
tom-designed wall of
laminated glass, the
lower level conference
room enjoys a partly
obscured view of the
stair.
Right: View of perimeter private offices seen
from beneath one of
the 10-ft. gypsum
board umbrella forms.

Left: A curved cherry space divider at the top of the stair.
Below: Upper level conference room has table and millwork of ebonized oak and shelving of clear-anodized aluminum.

269

TAS Design

Guggenheim Museum
Administrative Offices
New York, New York

The controversial addition to Frank Lloyd Wright's Guggenheim Museum solved some problems by adding new gallery space, but other problems remained. Some of these have been solved by TAS Design, and those solutions include the administrative office space shown here, carved from space below the sidewalk and plaza that surround the famous museum. Claustrophobia has been dispelled with skylights inserted into gardens at grade, with other circular openings that resemble skylights, with glass walls fronting private offices, and with a general openness of planning. The custom carpet, in soft autumn colors, recalls the pattern of Wright's terrazzo above, and angled space dividers echo the famous structure. Most visually dominant, however, lending a powerful character to the entire level and defining its circulation paths, is the great curved foundation wall of the museum itself. A difficult design assignment has produced a felicitous, functional and appropriately respectful result.

Above: Work surface detail of a custom desk design.
Below: Wall fronting private offices is of cherry, aluminum and glass.

Opposite: Open office areas lead to employee lounge. Carpet pattern recalls Wright's terrazzo design for the museum upstairs.
Photography: Paul Warchol

Above: Entrance to TAS Design's subterranean offices for the Guggenheim. Glass walls give a sense of light; round openings are taken from Wright.

Right: Dominating the lower level is the substantial curved foundation of the museum above.

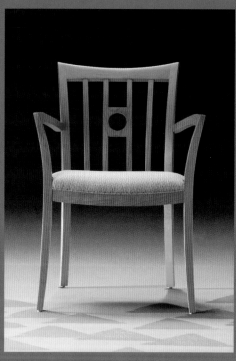

TERRANCE HUNT COLLECTION

TODAY, MORE THAN EVER BEFORE, THE PRODUCT WE SELECT AS CONSUMERS MUST BE EXPRESSIVE OF INDIVIDUAL TASTES, WORK WELL WITHIN ITS ENVIRONMENT, AND PROVE ITSELF AS A WORTHY INVESTMENT.

THROUGH DISTINCTIVE DESIGN, CABOT WRENN'S SEATING, LOUNGE, OCCASIONAL TABLES, AND CONFERENCE TABLES SUPPORT THE INTEGRITY OF TODAY'S BUSINESS INTERIORS. YOU CAN BE ASSURED, THAT THE CABOT WRENN

PRODUCT THAT YOU SELECT WILL PROVE ITSELF EFFECTIVE IN A VARIETY OF SETTINGS, WHILE ENDURING THE PASSAGES OF TIME.

CabotWrenn ®

P.O. Box 1763   Hickory, North Carolina 28603   704 495 460   704 495 4334 F

" This design is a unique connection of process, material and form. We found that with applied heat we were able to mold the fabric around a form. The more sculptural the form, the more the Xorel® responded. Xorel® gave the chair durability, beauty and comfort, while the chair illuminated the characteristics of Xorel®. The covering and the structure became one integral unit."

-Brian Kane
designer

XOREL CHAIR™

As the Xorel Chair™ fuses structure and material, so does it integrate the utility of a stacking chair with the elegance of an upholstered pull-up.

Xorel® fabrics are inherently flame retardant, cleanable and puncture proof. These qualities combine with the chair's strength, stacking ability and floating seat to make it ideal for hard use applications. Xorel's® nearly infinite possibilities for color, texture and pattern, and the chair's classic proportions and comfort make it appropriate for both corporate and institutional environments.

Included in the "International Design Yearbook"

Awarded the 1996 IIDA Apex Award
for Product Design

Carnegie
(800) 727-6770

Geiger BRICKEL

comprehensive

classic

distinctive

GEIGER BRICKEL HAS BUILT A REPU-
TATION AS ONE OF THE FINEST WOOD
OFFICE FURNITURE MANUFACTURERS
IN NORTH AMERICA SINCE 1964. WE
HAVE PROVIDED OUR CUSTOMERS WITH

CONTEMPORARY FURNISHINGS OF THE
HIGHEST INTERNATIONAL STANDARDS
IN QUALITY, DESIGN, CRAFTSMANSHIP,
VALUE, AND SERVICE. OUR MISSION:
TO KEEP PROMISES AND DELIVER
HIGH QUALITY PRODUCTS ON TIME.
PLEASE CALL 1.800.444.8812 TO FIND
THE GEIGER BRICKEL SALES REPRE-
SENTATIVE OR DEALER NEAREST YOU.

ANANAS

the symbol for hospitality.

A stylish new collection of fabrics from F.S. Contract

Good design is good business®

— Florence Knoll

Knoll

Easy Mood
designed by
Fernando Urquijo

Progetto 25
designed by
Luca Meda

Unifor, Inc.
149 Fifth Avenue
New York, NY 10010

Telephone: 212.673.3434
Facsimile: 212.673.7317
E-mail: unifor@uniforinc.com

Easy Mood
designed by
Fernando Urquijo

Progetto 25
designed by
Luca Meda

Unifor, Inc.
149 Fifth Avenue
New York, NY 10010

Telephone: 212.673.3434
Facsimile: 212.673.7317
E-mail: unifor@uniforinc.com

CONNECTIVES COLLECTION

Striking a Balance between Solid Wood Heritage and Modern Technology

SEROTINA COLLECTION

Wilsonart® Decorative Metals

Use The Smart Source To See More Of Yourself In Your Design.

We're providing new surfacing products — like A-Look Mirror Quality Decorative Metals — to help you turn your design ideas into reality. And that's another reason why Wilsonart International is known as The Smart Source.

For years, Wilsonart® Decorative Metals have helped you transform ordinary interiors into showplaces of light and color. Still, you probably think of them as a niche option.

Think again. Our new A-Look products make that niche look a whole lot bigger. These remarkable panels are not only lighter in weight than traditional mirrors, they're completely formable and never shatter or break. Offered in ten colors, designs and textures, they add a unique design element to many vertical and decorative accent applications — applications where maybe you would never have considered metals before.

The A-Look panels join our anodized aluminum and solid brass products to bring our complete metals line to 26 brilliant options. And more new designs are coming soon.

So call 800-433-3222 for literature, samples or more information. If you want your next project to reflect your very best thinking, they may be just the ticket.

Reflect on that.

Smart Surfaces

THE SMART SOURCE

WILSONART
I N T E R N A T I O N A L

Wilsonart® Laminate   Wilsonart® Custom Edges   Wilsonart® Solid Surfacing Veneer   Wilsonart® Gibraltar® Solid Surfacing

Use The Smart Source To Earn A New Degree Of Surface Versatility.

Wilsonart® Custom Laminate

Developing new surfacing options, and offering more of them than anybody else, is why Wilsonart International is known as The Smart Source.

Go to the source for the world's most popular laminate line, with 240 colors and designs. Wilsonart® Custom Edges, to give laminate countertops a custom look with no brown lines. Wilsonart® Decorative Metals, which can turn ordinary interiors into showplaces of light and color. Our newest product, Wilsonart® SSV™ Solid Surfacing Veneer, which creates the lavish look of solid surfacing more affordably. And Wilsonart® Gibraltar® Solid Surfacing in a new array of colors and patterns (including a full line of matching kitchen sinks and vanity bowls).

In fact, you can look to us for practically infinite options. Options for any design idea. Any performance requirement. Any budget. Add your imagination to the mix and that's one powerful combination.

So call 800-433-3222 for samples, our new Smart Source brochure and information on certified fabricators and installers in your area. You'll find that using The Smart Source is sort of like graduating to a new level of design success. You'll still be in class, though.

A class of your own.

Wilsonart® Gibraltar® Solid Surfacing

Smart Surfaces

THE SMART SOURCE

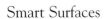

WILSONART
INTERNATIONAL

Wilsonart® Laminate   Wilsonart® Decorative Metals   Wilsonart® SSV™ Solid Surfacing Veneer   Wilsonart® Gibraltar® Solid Surfacing
Visit us at our website: http://www.builderonline.com/~wilsonart/

Westminster

...the solution for managers and others
who need orderly storage, adjustable keyboard components and versatile desk-mounted over-
heads. Unique components include a P-top worksurface, shown with articulating corner unit

Color

Endurance

The Next Level

Lees

DESIGN THAT MOVES YOU EVEN WHILE IT'S SITTING STILL.

You could be sitting on some of our best ideas. Design solutions for every seating application.
Executive. Managerial. Conference. Task. Guest. Stacking. From ergonomics to economics,
Vecta has a chair that will sit well with you.

VECTA

©1996 Vecta® Grand Prairie, Texas 75051

Tel 972 641 2860   Fax 972 660 1746

A Steelcase Design Partnership® company.

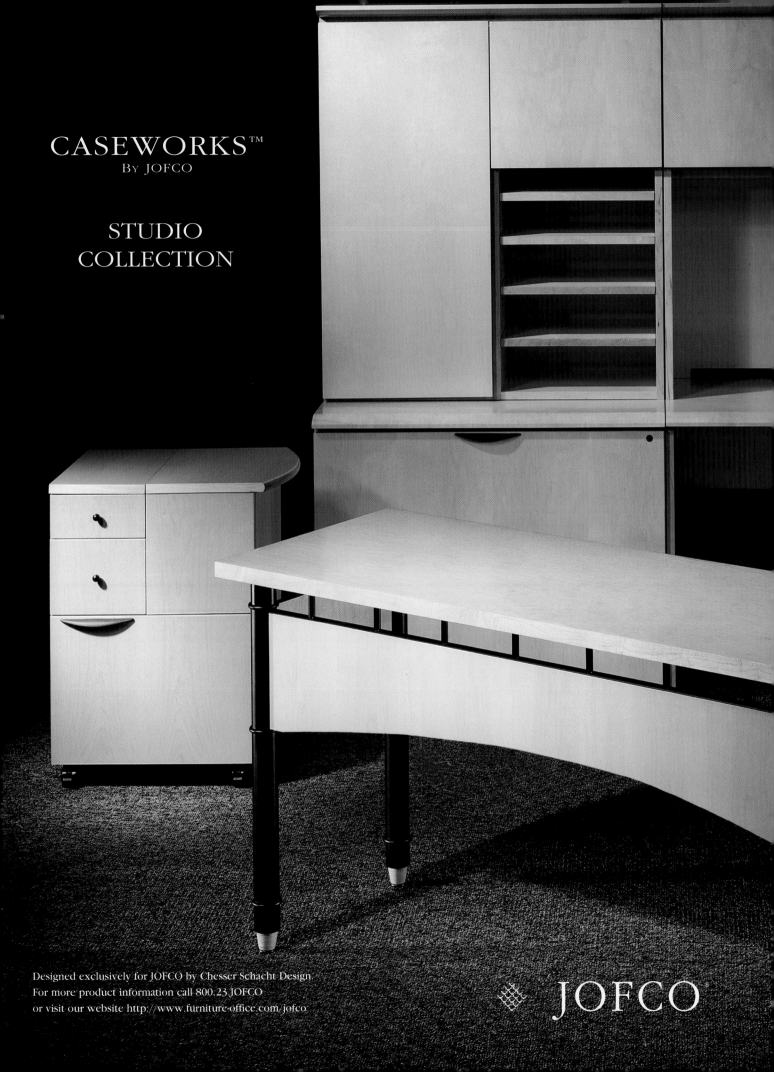

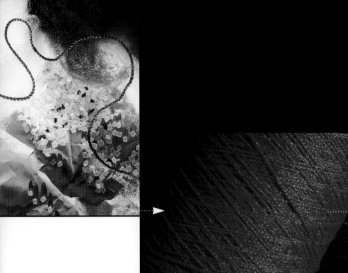

The thread of a great idea.

Designing a *flawless* interior evolves

from a moment of

inspiration followed by

impeccable attention to detail.

When your vision counts, explore **Monsanto**

Ultron® VIP premium nylon, Ultron® VIP Solution Dyed nylon and

Ultron® VIP FiberSet® nylon.

We'll give you the threads of your next *great idea*.

And *performance* that will floor you.

Monsanto Contract Fibers, 320 Interstate North Parkway, Atlanta, GA 30339 1-800-543-5377 or 1-770-951-7600

Interior design: Henry Goldston and Walt Thomas, AREA, Los Angeles; photo: Nick Merrick © Hedrich Blessing.

Imaginative design and superb performance begin with

the *Ultron*® *VIP* nylon

family of *premium* carpet fibers.

Your vision makes it possible. Our fibers make it happen.

ABOUT CHOOSING A DESIGN FIRM

Michael D. Tatum, IIDA

This volume is a feast for the eyes, and many of the workplaces depicted would be gratifying, productive and exciting places in which to spend one's workdays. Some of you may be contemplating the forthcoming design of your own offices, for which this is a terrific way to vicariously tour some of the finest work recently accomplished by truly excellent design organizations. If hiring a design firm is in your future, it will be far more rewarding if the process of doing so recognizes the complexities and realities you'll face. That will yield not only a far better result, but also a more pleasant, engaging, and fulfilling process. And the world of interior design and interior architecture is truly a magic and continually intriguing place, which continues to challenge and excite me daily after thirty-six years of doing it. Before we get into the "how to do it" stuff, let's review what you are and aren't trying to accomplish along with some salient realities that should affect your selection process.

What you're about to do is...

...enter into a professional relationship over a period of time.

...hire people — specific people with given levels of experience, sets of attitudes, abilities to present ideas, empathies with your situation, personality quirks.

...purchase *quality* of professional advice based upon *quality and nature* of experience.

...purchase *both quality and quantity* of people's time.

...enter into an *open and candid* information exchange over a period of time.

...try to satisfy the varied (*and often conflicting*) agendas of executive management, occupant management, facilities management and project management.

...maximize the positive *effects* of the professional service — which can far outweigh fees.

...hire professionals who know *a lot more* about their field of endeavor than you do (otherwise why bother?)

...purchase service which includes intensive personal contact and ongoing negotiation in your behalf.

...commission the solution of certain problems and/or the provision of certain services, both of which it is *your obligation* to *explicitly* define.

...attempt to compare professional organizations on an *apples-to-apples* basis.

...measure creativity, and capability and reliability *before the fact*.

What you're NOT about to do is...

...purchase *a uniform commodity* which can safely be bought on a "lowest price" basis. It's much closer to selecting an attorney, therapist or doctor than to purchasing pipe or paper.

...purchase something in which your organization will *not* participate.

...purchase all-encompassing services for a *fixed* low price.

...enter into a circumstance in which your organization will be invulnerable to *self-initiated* changes in scope of the work.

...trick anybody into providing unanticipated services without fee.

...purchase a "patsy" to relieve you of any potential culpability.

...try to bluff professional designers about how much you know about their game.

...get fooled by a "low ball", low fee, reduced scope proposal.

Realize that...

...the better and more candid the information design firms have about your organization and its situation, the better "match" you're likely to achieve between your needs and their capabilities.

...your organization's needs are probably not as unique as you think they are. Your particular *mixture* of needs may be unique, but the component parts are probably quite familiar to competent interiors firms.

...you are hiring *advocates for your cause*, and that your relationship with them can either enhance or dilute that advocacy in important ways that you can neither measure nor document.

...one piece of good advice given (or not) in a major lreal estate negotiation can far outweigh the entire professional fee.

...errors (or missed opportunities) in design, documentation or construction administration *which you may never find or see* can cost more than the entire design fee.

...the costs of change orders and scope changes *initiated by your organization* over the course of a project will usually far exceed the full "spread" of proposed fees.

The Patent Office was amazed. You will be, too.

"…it has enough technological materials and ergonomic breakthroughs to keep the patent office busy for weeks."

—Chee Perlman, Editor, *I.D.* Magazine

You're looking at the Aeron™ chair. It comes in three sizes to fit more people. Its innovative Pellicle™ suspension eliminates heat build-up and conforms to the unique shape of the person using it. Its innovative Kinemat™ tilt allows natural movement from forward-upright to reclining positions.

The Aeron chair. From Herman Miller, the world's leader in cross-performance work chairs.

herman miller

...the progressive approvals process is usual, and that you're responsible for all actions of the designers and contractors/suppliers based upon and following *each and every approval* you give.

...typically, substantive demands for wasteful "cover your ass" documentation and reports are made, which can and do *add very substantially* to fee costs.

...your own organization is probably neither as nimble nor as responsive as most capable design firms, and is likely to fall behind in supplying information.

...you're better served by being candid about how much you do and don't know. By admitting the extent of your ignorance, you'll probably gain valuable information.

What affects fees?

What key factors affect the cost of interior design services? While there are countless small contributors which are very difficult to define in advance, there are a few major predictable factors which you should define as carefully as possible before issuing the Requests for Proposals, or RFPs. If you need help defining them, ask the designers ahead of time. Most will willingly assist you, realizing that it will save them time in responding. Some of these factors are—

Scope of Services Required — Don't leave it vague. If you're asking for fee proposals, explicitly describe the services you need. Don't try to get something for nothing. The only firms that will give it to you are those that are terminally stupid or whose survival is in peril — and those probably aren't the safest ones to do your project.

Mix of Space Types Involved — This may be somewhat difficult to define quantitatively in advance of a completed Space Program. Nevertheless, give the best definition possible. You do know what <u>types</u> of spaces you'll need — and this may help respondents index their fees on a cost per square foot basis for each type of space. Common categories of space are —

"Typical" Office Space — This may be the lion's share of the project. It includes private offices, open office areas, conference and team rooms, departmental files, workrooms, and other such common office functions not covered in the following special categories.

High Finish Spaces — This includes those areas with more elegant finishes and appointments, which are much more time intensive that typical office spaces: Areas such as primary reception/conference, presentation rooms, executive offices, private dining rooms, special displays, some employee dining areas, fitness centers, retail banking halls, public lobbies.

High Technology Spaces — This includes those technology - intensive areas which substantially exceed the demands of typical spaces and are resultantly more time intensive: Areas such as computer rooms, laboratories, trading rooms, kitchens and servicing areas, "wet areas" in health facilities, medical areas, security centers, communications centers, teleconferencing rooms, photography studio/lab, video production centers.

Utilitarian Support Spaces — This includes those "basement like" utilitarian areas which may be less time intensive than typical office spaces: Areas such as paper and supplies storage, furniture storage, repair shops, mail processing, shipping/receiving.

Other Special Spaces — This includes special function areas which may not fit the above categories very tidily, such as day care centers, training centers, vendaterias, company stores.

Quantities of Space by Category — Okay, so maybe you haven't done a complete Space Program and you really aren't sure. Estimate the overall square footage (or range) as best you can, then assign approximate percentages to the above space categories, listing all the specific types of spaces within each category. If it's guesswork, just say so in the RFP. "Best guesses" are a lot better than no information at all.

Level of Demand for Time Intensive Services — If, for instance, you want each executive office individually designed, say so. That makes a big difference. And inventory, evaluation and reuse of varied existing furniture (when properly done) is usually more time-consuming than specifying new furniture. Multiple presentations of the layouts or designs, complex or multiple approvals processes, in-house education demands,

introducing

new age
comfort

WEBB
series

DAVIS

or special documentation needs should be made known to the designers as soon as you know about them.

Caution: Involve "amateurs with flair" in your decision-making at your own sometimes very costly peril. Whims have little place in the more structured and rationally-driven processes of contract interior design.

The following are key characteristics to look for among the design firm's team members. On a large project and with larger design firms you may have a Principal-In-Charge and a Design Principal as well as a Project Manager/Director and a Project Designer. In many cases *these roles may be combined*, particularly on smaller projects or by smaller firms.

The Principal-In-Charge represents extensive experience and the place the buck stops. This person should communicate effectively on a peer level with your leadership and should be able to create and maintain a bond of confidence and comfort with your executives on business issues. This person *probably won't have ongoing daily contact* with your project staff.

The Design Principal represents senior, experienced design leadership and should be able to describe design concepts, determinants and other esthetic issues in clear and comforting business terms with your leaders. This person probably won't have a lot of ongoing daily contact with your project staff.

The Project Manager/Director is the "hub" of the project, and as such, should show clear signs of leadership and command of the process. This person should be able to communicate effectively with all your people involved in your project. The Project Manager is the person with whom your project staff is likely to have the greatest ongoing contact.

The Project Designer leads the design staff in generating the conceptual plans and esthetic ideas for the project and should be able to effectively discuss issues of both substance and style with virtually anyone and everyone in your organization.

The Project Architect — If your project's technical development lies months in the future, this person may not be named at the time of selection. But this person, usually not in an intensive client contact role, is critical to control of quality, costs and errors on your project. In this role, presentation skills don't count much

— but experience, knowledge and gritty determination count for a lot.

Which team seems to empathize best with your group's collective and individual aspirations, goals and concerns? Who best sees things your way? With which group did you feel most/least comfortable? Comfort, empathy and confidence are important ingredients to a pleasant and effective project relationship.

"Time, Cost, Quality," says the maxim, "Pick *any two*. They'll determine the third." True in many aspects of life, including interior design.

Want quality very fast? Plan on *paying well* for it.
Want quality on a budget? It'll take *plenty of time* and focus.
Want it both fast and cheap? *Don't* expect much quality.

Truly clever and capable designers can hedge these probabilities somewhat, but they cannot overcome these inevitable tendencies. About these issues...

Time—Yesterday's "fast track" schedules are today's norms. Still, inadequate time will cost you money, quality or both. Ideally, you want to move as fast as possible without using *any* of your budget to buy *only time*. Ask leading designer candidates what's reasonable in terms of schedule. They'll each bracket what's best from their viewpoints.

Cost—Again, if you can describe what you'd like to accomplish functionally, what organizational qualities you'd like to portray, what unseen technology infrastructure you need, candidate designers will be happy to counsel you about construction, furnishings and fee budgets. If you're looking for a budget project, search for designers whose forte is low-budget work. Some only do expensive work, some a full range, some thrive on the challenge of low budgets. And *don't* look for lowest fees for low budget projects. The extra clever consideration afforded by an extra dollar a square foot in design fees may leverage the *impression of* an extra five to ten dollars a foot in the project's effect.

Quality doesn't equate with opulence. Opulence is waste, and even in high-budget, high-finish work, you (and a quality designer) will want to squeeze every dime's worth of value out of your expenditures. Quality, if sought and nurtured, can be delivered on

Not just for today.

HALLER SYSTEMS™

Anyone who is interested in the principle "Form follows function" loves forms that last a small eternity. Forms that remain valid for a long time and are free of superfluous paraphernalia. KITOS, the Complex Integrated Table Organization System is designed with this principle in mind. With KITOS you can become a role model. Not just today.

We shall be happy to send you further information. Just call **1-800-4 HALLER** and quote the following reference No.: KB1

U. Schaerer Sons Inc.
A & D Building
150 East 58th Street
New York, N.Y. 10155
Telephone: 212 371 1230
Telefax: 212 371 1251

Mobili G Inc.
Showplace Design Center #341
2 Henry Adams Street
San Francisco, CA 94103
Telephone: 415 431 9900
Telefax: 415 431 9901

even the low budget projects. Quality in finished projects derives from the quality of the people you engage, and the compensated time necessary for them to create with thorough consideration and care—so it is *not* achievable for "low-ball" design fees.

THE SCOPE OF SERVICE YOU SEEK

Even for seemingly similar projects, the scope of design services may be *vastly different.* Organizations *vary substantially* in what services fall under the 'umbrellas' of "design". Here is a very brief and broad overview of the key categories of services:

Pre-Design Special Services—such as *truly strategic* facilities plans, "alternative officing" studies, real-estate search assistance, problem identification audits, trends analyses, change readiness assessments, special financial analyses, et cetera, which are <u>not</u> part of any design organization's "basic or usual" design services.

Facility Programming—At progressively greater levels of detail: "broad brush" information supportive of real estate searches or "shell and core" design of buildings; followed by a detailed accounting of people, 'stuff' and spaces by sizes and types to support layouts and design work; then followed by fully detailed requirements for construction, engineering/technologic needs, and furnishings/finishes.

Preliminary Planning/Conceptual Design—Developed in parallel, preliminary space layouts show interior architectural features and furnishings, and are accompanied by sketches and materials/color palettes depicting design intent.

Final Planning/Detailed Design—complete interior architectural and furnishings drawings, engineering considerations specific assignment of all materials and colors preparatory to contract documents.

Contract Documents—Working drawings, construction/materials/furnishings specifications as required for bidding and implementation.

Bidding, Negotiation—Receipt of bids, or negotiation of prices and contractual conditions through execution of contracts.

Contract Administration—Representation of your interests in achieving the intent of your contract documents through construction, manufacturing, installation.

Finishing Touches—Not usually part of *basic* design services, this includes selection and placement of art, accessories and plants, and execution or coordination of architectural signage/graphics.

Optional Services—These can cover a broad range from extra renderings and models, to special economic analyses, pre/post-occupancy evaluations, and a range of special consultation or its coordination, as well as ongoing facility management services.

FORMAT OF YOUR REQUEST FOR PROPOSAL

If there are very special characteristics you need to express and/or which need response, treat them as such in a separate section of the RFP. Insofar as possible, *avoid* quirky or very unusual formats — you'll get better responses that way. Most design firms are prepared to respond to repetitive issues in a fairly common format, and you should take advantage of that. Many design firms consider arbitrarily restructured RFP formats as a sign of potential problems on a project — and they're often correct.

The following is a suggested structure for your RFP which will probably be familiar to most design firms.

1. **History/Background** — I'll show you mine if you'll show me yours.

2. **Summary Overview of Project** — You state it, they confirm understanding.

3. **Project Scope** — How big, where located, what mix of space types, what quality level desired.

4. **Scope of Services** — What do you think you'll need? Proposal based upon that with their observations of alternative or additional services.

5. **Priorities** — A brief description, in order of importance, of your current priorities. Ask them to respond specifically to each.

6. **Schedule** — Briefly describe the anticipated schedule (and what's driving it) and ask them to provide a detailed bar chart schedule of their work based upon your needs.

7. **Project Organization Structure** — Show them your team structure. They'll respond with theirs.

8. **Key Personnel** — Ask for biographies of their key team members, descriptions of the roles of each and personal references for each person performing in that role.

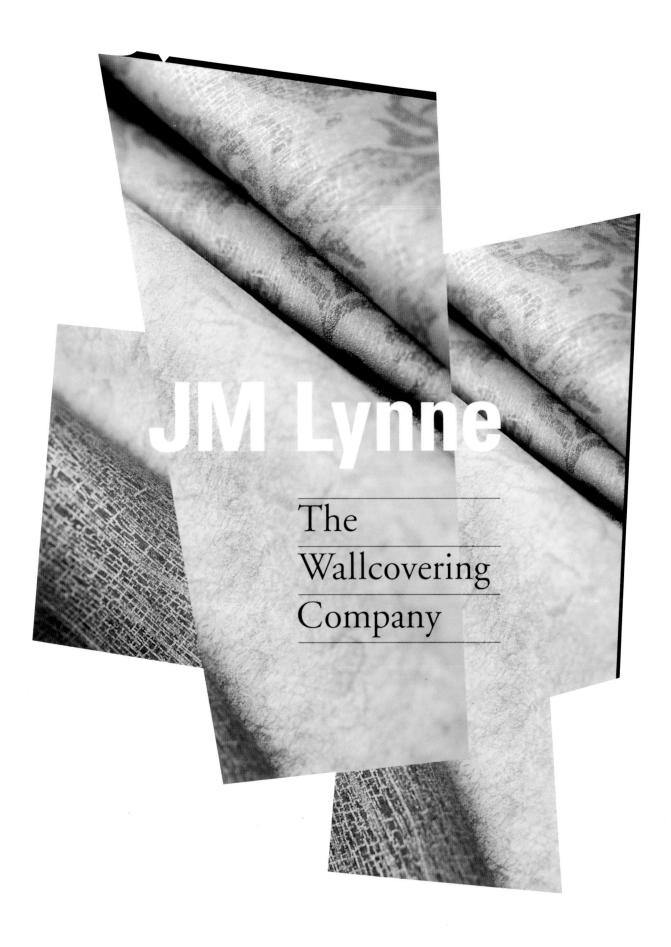

JM Lynne

The
Wallcovering
Company

Shown: *Fresco/Mimosa Series Commercial Vinyl Wallcovering*
Design: *Patty Madden*
For more information: 800 645 5044

9. **Applicable Experience/ References** — Ask for specifically applicable experience as well as for a long list that they can't pre-qualify. For each project, which of their people were in key roles?

10. **Locational Accessibility** — How conveniently located are they in relationship to occupant groups (for programming and space plan reviews), to project management groups (for ongoing coordination) and to the project location (for construction administration)? Ask that they estimate cost of travel reimbursables, if applicable.

11. **Process Description** — Ask them to tell you a story about how they'll do your work.

12. **Specific Questions, Critical Issues** — Assuming you've already done your homework, ask about your major concerns quite candidly. The responses should be a good "sorter".

13. **Compensation** — Ask for a fee proposal on a specific basis; entertain alternative bases of compensation for comparative consideration.

14. **Special Qualifications** — Why are they the best-suited design organization to respond to your specific project needs?

Describing Your Current Circumstances — Let the prospective designers know the following, unless there's very substantive reason not to do so: Describe the extent to which you've done a Space Program and make the results available to them for review. If you've selected a site, building architect or existing building, tell them about it. If the project's occupants are now in 7 widely dispersed locations, let them know. Don't surprise them later with a 3-layer approvals process. Don't tell them later that they cannot present their design proposals directly to your executive decision-makers (which, incidentally is a deplorably counter-productive practice). If you have a very short time schedule or have a lease agreement that demands working drawings far ahead of occupancy, let them know. Offer to let them tour existing facilities and tell them what is and isn't satisfactory about them. Be candid about what quality level you're shooting for. Let them know what your in-house project staff can and cannot do.

Their Control Over Implementation — Can you pre-qualify contractors? Are you "locked in" to a particular construction or furnishings contractor? Must you accept, or do you usually accept the low bid? Will the designer have clear control over quality during construction? Contractors' performance can very strongly affect the designer's contract administration costs — as much as by *several hundred percent* if a contractor is particularly incompetent or uncooperative. If the designer has reasonable control of contractor selection, this can be moderated and the designer held responsible — but if contractors are forced upon the designer, the designer could be at substantial risk of losing money due to selections made by others. If a contractor's performance is highly questionable in advance or in process, have the designer keep track of the excess time demanded by that contractor's poor performance. Then at the end of the project, you may go to the real source of the problem (the contractor) to recoup the extra contract administration costs you've suffered because of their inadequate performance.

Concerns About Computer Capabilities — Do you really need computer-assisted space programming (probably), computer assisted design and drafting (probably), computer based facilities management information (possibly)? If so, find out the following about each:

-Whose software and hardware are used for each system? Has it been modified by them?

-How many local staff are currently using the system, their names, dates they completed training?

-How long has such a system been operational at the location where your work will be executed?

-Do associate engineers use *a compatible CAD system* to allow complete drawing integration? Specifications integration? -Describe interactivity of programming/planning/design/engineering systems, if existent.

Other important information to include in your RFP includes:

Your Decision-Making Process — Tell them who will participate in the final selection of the designer, what the key interests of each person are, and your selection timetable. This will help each design firm present their capabilities more effectively and more concisely — but still from an equal base of information.

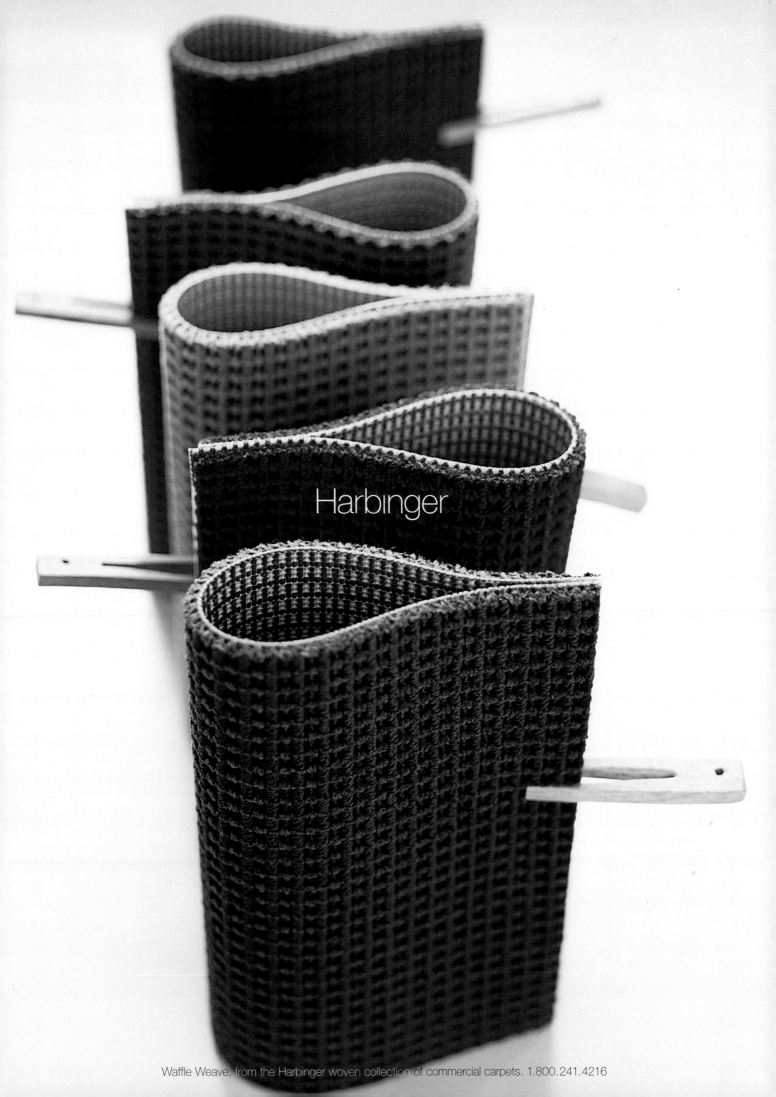

Harbinger

Waffle Weave, from the Harbinger woven collection of commercial carpets. 1.800.241.4216

Your Expected Fee Structure — If you have very firm scopes of service and area definitions and feel very comfortable about the project's general stability, you may ask for a fixed fee. If only the amount of space is variable, you may want a fixed overall fee *per square foot*. If the overall amount and the mix of types of spaces is variable, you may want a *fee per square foot for each category of space type*. If there's substantial uncertainty, an hourly rate basis with or without an estimated maximum may be the best route. If you feel a particular design firm may take unfair advantage of an hourly open-end situation, don't hire 'em — the element of trust is important. In any case, determine the hourly rate basis for additional services and the markup (if any) on reimbursable expenses, as well as what's included in reimbursable expenses. Realize that, particularly if travel is involved, reimbursable expenses can be quite substantive.

Incentives to Save Fee — In most hourly rate fee structures, the designer has little or no incentive to save fee. In an "hourly with a fixed maximum" structure (which fewer and fewer designers will accept), the designer loses if the maximum is exceeded, but gets nothing extra for staying well under the maximum. Some sort of "split the difference" incentive for significant fee savings can work to your advantage — and it gives your organization an incentive to handle *your end of it* in a lean, effective manner.

Requests for References — In addition to requesting a list of "Applicable Experience/References" (if they're smart, you'll of course get only their best), you may want to ask for a list of *all projects completed by that office* within a certain size range on given schedules (if that's a significant issue) within the last 2-5 years. Then you can call a few at random to see how their performance references hold up.

PRIORITIES/ANTI-PRIORITIES

The late Buckminster Fuller once observed that "You cannot select a priority without implicitly admitting an anti-priority". Like it or not, everything can't be a top priority. Be alert to the anti-priorities which accompany each priority you select. The old saw about anti-priorities says, "Cost. Quality. Time. Select any two and they will define the third." and there are very definite limits beyond which you can't cheat that equation.

REVIEWING THE PROPOSALS

If proposals are received ahead of interviews (they should be) and are thoroughly reviewed prior to presentation/interviews, you will be able to ask incisive questions about specific points of concern in each — and incisive, intelligent questions are your best tool in personal presentations/interviews. It's best to go over proposals twice. First, review them for finite information. That will tell you what questions and concerns remain unanswered. Note them. Then scan all proposals again, perhaps on a section-by-section comparative basis, to develop a concept of how they compare to each other. In doing both comparisons, focus *at least* upon the following issues.

Structure/Format — Does it parallel your RFP for ease of analysis? Is it clear in its organization? Is it easy to find the information you're looking for? It may foretell the clarity of project design presentations.

Responsiveness/Thoroughness — Is it responsive to your "need to know". Is the information presented focused upon your interests? How does its completeness compare with other proposals?

Experience — How does their relevant experience compare? Do they have experience in all the important component parts of your project? Are there apparent gaps in experience that you need to investigate?

Personnel — For their key team members, what is their average number of years of professional experience? How long has each been with that firm? Have they worked together (either as a team, or in various combinations) before?

Design — Do their projects tend to look alike? If so, is that what we want? If not, do any of them come close to what we want — or might we be missing the target just by chance? Don't be scared by the apparent cost of what you see until you confirm that it's too expensive for you (good designers can stretch budgets). How many of the projects have been done *by your proposed project designer*?

Reliability — Do their descriptions of project processes seem clear and convey competence? References might as well be wallpaper unless they're called. Try to contact past projects that aren't on the project reference list, too. Find out from the person who gives the reference their role on the project. If they had no active role in the project, seek someone else. Monday-morning quarterbacks aren't any more helpful than sour grapes are tasty. Be sure to try to sort out failures of contractors or suppliers from failures of the design firm.

s e r r a

design: paul james | mehmet ergelen

Schedule — Do they have substantive "fast track" experience (a test of fire for reliability)? Have they met schedule responsibilities reliably? Does their proposed schedule look well-constructed, comprehensive? How does it compare with competitors' schedules?

Productivity/Economic Issues — Which organization best addresses those issues that affect your workers' productivity? Which one best addresses control of costs, "dollar stretching" via design ingenuity, error reduction, lease conditions/work letters, and other important economic factors?

DIFFERENT AUDIENCES, DIFFERENT PLAYERS — In any sizable business organization, yours included, there are several constituencies with different priorities and attitudes. Any experienced business design organization realizes that fact, and tries to adapt to it. You should realize, as well, that your top executives, facilities managers, purchasing agents, real estate specialists, occupant/management and clerical occupants have widely varying (and often conflicting) priorities. It is important that the design team be able to deal effectively with each of these constituencies, for it is only in that way that broad acceptance of working environments is created.

STYLE AND SUBSTANCE — Design organizations vary considerably in their viewpoints, priorities, beliefs and motivations. As I will describe each, I'm describing relative tendencies, not finite or exclusive characteristics. But, in each case Bucky Fuller's admonition that "you cannot select a priority without implicitly admitting an anti-priority" applies.

The "style camp" generally describes those design organizations which place a very high priority upon their own identifiable esthetic style or styles. Conversely, issues of business substance tend to take a lower priority. Style oriented firms may have a very narrow single style or somewhat more variety, but the appearance of their work will tend to be somewhat predictable. If this is the kind of firm you seek, be sure that what you see satisfies your desires, because you're unlikely to change the design firm's philosophy during the course of your project.

The "substance camp" generally describes those organizations which place a very high priority upon issues of business substance such as operational effectiveness, budgets and schedules. Conversely, they will tend to have less stringent views of style and esthetics. Among such firms, you may find a very broad range of stylistic

expressions. If this is the type of firm you seek, <u>don't</u> assume that the range of styles you see in a presentation is all encompassing. It may be their best guess of what they think you want based upon inadequate information. In this case, it's more likely that specific projects' appearances represent the desires or characteristics of those specific clients.

DESIGN TECHNOLOGY—A TOOL, NOT A SOLUTION

Be particularly alert to those who "shovel smoke". Many command the buzzwords and have learned to feign technologic capacities which are largely fiction. At the same time, don't over-emphasize its importance to you. If you know how their technologic prowess can specifically support your needs in critical ways, insist upon it. Otherwise, judge primarily upon effective overall results rather than upon flashy techniques and buzzwords. *Look for hard evidence.*

THEIR PRESENTATION/INTERVIEW

It's a good idea to receive Statements of Qualifications (essentially Proposals without fee sections) or Proposals (with fees included) prior to conducting your "short list" interviews. Some clients will conduct abbreviated interviews of their "long list" of as many as six to ten design firms. Others will receive proposals, select a "short list" of two to four design firms and interview only those. Do whichever gives you sufficient comfort.

You've allowed an hour and a half or more for each presentation/interview, *all* your team members will be present and well-prepared, having reviewed the proposals and prepared their questions *in advance*. The task ahead is to assess the people who'll do your work, the human spirit of each organization, and to do so in as orderly and complete a manner as time allows.

Ask questions of those presenting. Don't be afraid of showing your ignorance of their business. Eventually, they'll have to overcome their initial ignorance of the specifics of your business. This is an excellent opportunity for you and your team to learn. Ask some of the same questions of each group, comparing both the content and attitudes of the responses. Some of the more naive, "off the wall" questions may be most revealing, since they're likely to call upon extemporaneous responses from depth of experience, along with some tact and grace. When in doubt, pursue the answer till you're satisfied.

CARRARA

Utilizing distinctive sloping edges and a centered concave reveal, the Carrara Collection by Gianni blends contemporary and classic design elements with functionality and superb workmanship. Designed by Salvatore Graziano and Mark Stenftenagel, the Carrara Collection is available in a full range of components and in a wide variety of woods and finishes. Contact Gianni for more information.

Photography: George Lambros

GIANNI

4615 West Roosevelt Road Cicero, IL 60650-1522 • 708.863.6696 • 1.800.237.0847

EVALUATING THEIR PEOPLE

As you listen to both their prepared presentations and their responses to questions, ask yourself some of the following general questions about each team member.

Will I enjoy spending a significant amount of time (to the extent that it's applicable) working with this person over the next several months? You're entering into a personal relationship and should feel comfortable with it. Test, then trust your instincts.

> Do I believe this person will not, under any conditions, let me down?

> Do they seem to relate effectively to their counterparts on our team?

> Does each team member communicate his/her role or message effectively, concisely?

> Do they appear to listen well, to question and interpret your meanings with accuracy?

> Do they seem candid and open, or protective and closed in the way they present, and discuss matters?

> Does each person's personal presentation indicate or exceed the expectations which their biographies raise?

PROBING THE WEAKNESSES

We haven't yet discussed some of the negatives you may anticipate. And since you may safely assume that the design world works on the same bell curve of competence as the rest of the world, there are bound to be some negatives. For the sake of brevity and to avoid depressing you before you start, I'll just mention a few of the more chronic ills to which you should be alert.

> Some designers have little or no understanding (or interest) in the business world, to the point that they have difficulty understanding or interpreting business priorities.

> Some designers do not structure project decision-making information in ways that are clear to business persons. (ask for samples.)

> Some don't clearly understand how management concepts or business practices relate to environmental elements, costs and consequences. (Search for evidence.)

> Some are strongly swayed by currently popular esthetic trends and will tend to produce anonymous, trendy, dated designs. (Look at some earlier work.)

COMPARING THE COMPETITORS

It will be helpful if you have some aids to evaluation, such as...

... lists of characteristics you're seeking for each aspect of the proposed presentation, perhaps with an evaluation scale to be marked for each.

... lists of questions for which you need answers with a place for individual evaluation of the answers.

... consolidation sheets, so that you can "spreadsheet" your comparative evaluations.

... pre-scheduled comparison/discussion/decision conferences *immediately following* the presentations.

You may want to statistically compare evaluation, but I caution against selecting a design firm "by the numbers". It makes no more sense than selecting an accountant on the basis of the stylishness of his or her attire. Discuss it as thoroughly as seems reasonable, then select your winner. As soon as your contract negotiations are reasonably firm, notify the "also-rans" and debrief them candidly on their efforts.

A GOOD BEGINNING

A redesign or relocation project is, at any scale, a major undertaking. It is very complex, but it's the everyday work of design firms such as you see herein. This may seem a significant investment of time just to select a design firm to begin the work. That's true. But to shortcut this beginning, to make the wrong selection, will ultimately prove far more costly in terms of quality dollars and time. Having prepared and selected well supports your peace of mind and satisfaction throughout the design process, and for years thereafter.

Michael D. Tatum, IIDA has designed interior work environments for over 30 years, in the course of which he has directed the design of more than 20 million square feet of contract interiors.

He now consults with both design firms and their clients as well as serving on the faculty of the Interior Design Program of the School of Architecture at the University of Texas at Arlington.

Agra. 1900 circa. 11.6x18.4 feet.

DARIUS

Distinguished antique and decorative rugs
SINCE 1885

38 East 57th Street   New York, New York 10022   (212) 644-6600

INDEX BY PROJECTS